The church from the South-west, *c.* 1830, from a painting by John Taylor.

THE PARISH CHURCH
OF ST. THOMAS À BECKET

CHAPEL-EN-LE-FRITH

1225—1925

THE PARISH CHURCH

OF

ST. THOMAS À BECKET

CHAPEL-EN-LE-FRITH

1225—1925

BY
WM. BRAYLESFORD BUNTING
Member of the Derbyshire Archæological and Natural History Society

MANCHESTER
SHERRATT & HUGHES
1925

Copyright © 1925 William Braylesford Bunting

ISBN: 978-1-913725-10-5

First published in 1925 by Sherratt & Hughes, Manchester.
This paperback edition published in 2025 by Nigel Gourlay, Ashworth House, Long Lane, Chapel-en-le-Frith, High Peak, SK23 0TF.
email: ngourlay@gmail.com

PREFACE.

SOME thirty years ago when the Church of St. Thomas à Becket was being carefully restored the writer was led to make notes of some features brought to light and to study the church's history. Some of these notes were communicated to the local Parish Magazine, but always with the hope that at a future time a more full and connected record might be published. The time now seems opportune for—although the celebration of the seven hundredth anniversary of an English parish church may in itself be scarcely worthy of notice from the point of view of antiquity—the circumstances of its foundation and its subsequent history, particularly with regard to the right of presentation to the benefice encourage the hope that a short account of the church may not prove unacceptable.

This is in no sense a history of the parish of Chapel-en-le-Frith and whilst, naturally, the story of an ancient parish church and of the parish attached to it must be closely interwoven, no attempt has been made in the following pages to trace the history of the parish as a whole.

It is to be hoped that some day a more able pen may undertake this interesting task for which ample material is available.

One word to the courteous critic. It will no doubt be observed by some that the writer is too fond of saying " it appears," " probably," and so on and is seldom sure of his ground. He is *not* always sure of his ground. The writer's researches convince him that too often the enthusiastic local historian seizes on a " half truth " and, without duly weighing the evidence or verifying the authority, adopts the statement as a "whole truth." Guide books and Directories follow suit and the half truth is accepted as fact until some more careful investigator or more competent antiquarian explodes the story with perhaps contempt or scorn. Without going far from home the pleasing story of Dorothy Vernon's steps may be taken as an example and a warning. The writer has tried, he hopes, if not always successfully, at least conscientiously, to avoid this deadly sin and to state as fact only what he has good reason to believe to be fact.

The writer's acknowledgments are due to Mr. Ernest Bagshawe, J.P., of Ford Hall, for permission to publish the plan of the church and churchyard in 1702, and to use the Diary of Dr. James Clegg. The latter, a daily chronicle of local doings carefully kept, throws, as will be seen in the following pages, much interesting light on church life in the parish in the first half of the eighteenth century.

He would also acknowledge his indebtedness to the standard works on *The Churches of Derbyshire* and its sister volumes *Three Centuries of Derbyshire Annals*, edited by the late Rev. J. Charles Cox, and also for notes given to him by Dr. Cox in later years : to the writers of numerous articles in the Derbyshire Archæological Society's Journal; to Mr. Edward G. Bagshawe of Sheffield; to the Vicar and Churchwardens of the parish for permission to examine the parochial documents; to many parishioners past and present for much valuable assistance and information (and particularly to the late Mrs. Frank Butler for the use of the painting on which our frontispiece is founded; to Col. Goodman, C.B., D.L., of Eccles House, Mr. Henry Kirke, M.A., the late Mr. W. H. Greaves Bagshawe, J.P., D.L., and the late Mr. J. C. Hyde), also to the Deputy Keeper of H.M. Record Office for permission to reproduce the Elizabethan plan of Chapel-en-le-Frith, to Professor A. C. Dickie of Victoria University, Manchester, to Mr. T.

Marsland for photographs and sketches, to Ferodo, Ltd., of Chapel-en-le-Frith, for help with the illustrations, to Mr. H. E. Walker for assistance in checking proofs, etc., and to Mr. W. C. Wynn, of Whaley Bridge, for the excellent reproduction of the picture forming the frontispiece and for photographs.

CHAPEL-EN-LE-FRITH,
    February, 1925.

CONTENTS.

CHAP.		PAGE
I.	Introductory	1
II.	The Church of St. Thomas à Becket	9
III.	The Men of Bowden and their Chapel	36
IV.	The Tithes of the Peak Forest and the Chaplains' Income	51
V.	The Parishioners' Right of Presentation	62
VI.	The Chaplains or Ministers	78
VII.	The Church Officials	85
VIII.	The Parish Registers	110
IX.	Pews and Burials in the Church	121
X.	The Bells and Ringers	132
XI.	Music and Singing	137
XII.	Miscellanea	146
	Index	159

ILLUSTRATIONS.

The Church from the South-west, c. 1830, from a painting by John Taylor ... ... *Frontispiece*
(*Photographed by Mr. W. C. Wynn.*)

Facing page

The Chancel in 1890, before restoration, from a contemporary photograph 9
(*Photographed by Mr. W. C. Wynn.*)

The Church and Town from an Elizabethan Map of the Peak Forest 18
(*Copied by Mr. T. Marsland.*)

Interior of the Church from S.W. 21
(*Photograph by Mr. W. C. Wynn.*)

The Stone Coffin 28
(*From a Sketch by Mr. T. Marsland.*)

"The Woodman's Axe" 30
(*From a Sketch by Mr. T. Marsland.*)

Plan of Graves in Church and Churchyard, 1709 ... *at end*

"*If I have done well and as is fitting, it is that which I desired; but if slenderly and meanly it is that which I could attain unto.*"

CHAPTER I.

INTRODUCTORY.

THE FOREST OF HIGH PEAK.

FAR back in the dim ages of the world's early history wild animals made a beaten trackway from South-Western Yorkshire to the salt marshes where is now the Cheshire plain—later on this old track was trodden by the feet of neolithic man whose traces may be found in the Tumuli of Lord's Seat, Greenlow and Cadster. They or their descendants perhaps worshipped the Sun God, for not far away is the Bull Ring at Dove Holes, contemporary with and closely resembling Stonehenge, but they unconsciously prepared the way for the Christian Church of which the following pages give an account. This prehistoric trackway is one of several followed and adapted by succeeding races of men, converging on an Upland valley in what was to become the Forest of High Peak, and here at the junction of these old ways was built in the thirteenth century a Chapel of Ease which in time became known as the Parish Church of Chapel-en-le-Frith.

To appreciate how this came about we must briefly glance at the history of the "King's Forest of High Peak." At the time of the Norman Conquest, and probably for some centuries earlier, the north-western portion of Derbyshire, covering some forty square miles, was the patrimony of the English Kings and formed the forest area: the term "forest" does not necessarily connote a wide space covered by great trees, but is used to designate a Royal hunting ground.

The forest area comprised in part what are now the

parishes of Hope, Glossop and Chapel-en-le-Frith. We are told in Domesday that there was a church and priest at Hope, but no other church within the forest precincts is mentioned. It does not, however, necessarily follow that there was no other church, as in some instances churches not noticed in Domesday are known to have existed. The ecclesiastical parish of Hope is to this day very extensive, and it would seem that at the date of the Survey (which was completed in 1086) the whole of the forest was tacitly, if not actually, within the district served by the Priest of Hope.

We also learn from Domesday that "The whole of Langdendale is waste. Wood(land) is there not for pannage (but) suitable for hunting." Langdendale is believed to have included that part of the forest abutting on the River Goyt between Marple Bridge on the one hand, and, probably, the upper end of the present parish of Fernilee on the other, and this included the district a little later known as Bowden, part of which now forms the parish of Chapel-en-le-Frith.[1]

We may gather from Domesday that this area was in the latter half of the eleventh century practically devoid of human life save perhaps for a few foresters and huntsmen.

We do not know if or when the parish of Castleton—which is said to have once included Glossop—became detached from Hope, but we do know that at the end of the twelfth century part of Bowden, Fernilee, Wormhill and Tideswell were all considered as being within the jurisdiction of the Church of Hope.

---

1. The Rev. C. Kerry says Langdendale included the whole parish of Glossop (*Derbys. Arch. Socy's. Jour.*, xv., p. 67). The writer suggests that its Eastern boundary extended from the Goyt at Fernilee along the line of Crosses: the Ladys, Martinside, Peaslows and Swyer Crosses to the Edale Cross below Kinder. A note on the Elizabethan plan mentioned on p. 18 suggests that Chapel-en-le-Frith parish was then considered to be within the "Champion" Division of the Forest.

Of the 162 Manors bestowed by William the Conqueror on his favourite—and as some say, erroneously, his natural son—William Peverel, the famous Peverel of the Peak, the Manor of High Peak was one. When, in expiation of a brutal murder, the great estates of the Peverels were escheated to the Crown in the reign of Henry II, that King granted the Manor of High Peak to his second son John, Earl of Mortaigne, afterwards King John, and it remained part of the royal demesne until the end of the reign of Edward III, by whom it was bestowed on his fourth son, John of Gaunt, Duke of Lancaster, and thus became absorbed into the Duchy which to this day claims mineral and other rights in the High Peak.

William, son of Peverel of the Peak, founded a Premonstratentian Priory—an offshoot of the great Abbey of Clugny—at Lenton near Nottingham, and according to the foundation charter quoted by Dugdale he gave to the Priory two-thirds of the tithes of the pastures pertaining to his Lordships in the Peak, including amongst other places Shallcross, Fernilee and one or two places that are not now to be identified : also the whole tithe of colts and fillies, wherever he had a stable (*haracium*) in the Peak, and the whole tithes of lead and hunting.

John, Earl of Mortaigne, in 1192, granted the Church of Hope with its Chapelry of Tideswell to the Bishop of Coventry and Lichfield and his successors. Subsequent bishops, including Alexander de Stavenby, of whom we shall hear more later, transferred their rights in the Church of Hope to the Dean and Chapter of Lichfield, who still hold the patronage of the benefice.

When we come to examine the claims to the right of presentation to Chapel Church we shall see the important bearing of these transactions upon the question. The piety or policy of the younger Peverel and of the Earl of Mortaigne engendered a long series of quarrels throughout the Middle Ages which reacted on the right of the parishioners of Chapel-en-le-Frith to select their minister, a right finally established by the great law-suit of *Thornhill* v. *Tooker* in the reign of James I.

The claims to the ownership of the tithes of the parish are clearly referable to these grants, and this is in itself evidence that the portion of Bowden now comprising Chapel-en-le-Frith parish was in the twelfth century considered, and was later admitted, to be in the ancient parish of Hope.

The Feast of the Translation of St. Thomas of Canterbury.

On Tuesday, the 29th December, 1170, the great Archbishop Thomas à Becket was murdered in his Cathedral Church of Canterbury, and three years later he was canonised as a saint. His body lay in the crypt for half a century till on Tuesday, the 7th July, 1220, it was removed with every mark of pomp and reverence to the Shrine near to the High Altar and to the Eastward of the Patriarchal Chair, there to remain until the Shrine was demolished at the Reformation.

The day was enrolled amongst the Great Festivals of the English Church as " The Feast of the Translation of St. Thomas of Canterbury." Then began the long succession of pilgrimages which for three centuries gave Canterbury a place amongst the great resorts of Christendom. As says Chaucer :—

" . . . . from every shire's end
Of England, to Canterbury they wend,
The holy blisful martyr for to seek,"

and it may be that men from the distant Forest of the High Peak had made the journey.

THE FEAST OF THE TRANSLATION

The late Dean Stanley suggests[1] that Tuesday was undoubtedly chosen in that age of ceremonial observance as being peculiarly significant in Becket's life. He was born and baptised on a Tuesday, on a Tuesday he fled from Northampton, on a Tuesday he left England on his exile, on a Tuesday he received warning of his martyrdom in a vision at Pontigny, on a Tuesday he returned from that exile and, as we have seen, on a Tuesday he was murdered also (as the next generation observed) it was on a Tuesday that his enemy Henry II was buried.[2]

Dr. Cox gives the date of the foundation of our Church as "about 1225." The men of Bowden when they built their chapel were "up-to-date," and dedicated it to the latest and no doubt at the time the most popular saint in the Kalendar, St. Thomas of Canterbury.

The first occasion after the Translation on which the 7th July fell on a Tuesday was in 1226, and, whilst the historian must not indulge in poetic license, we think it is not unfair to suggest that the building—which tradition says was a small one—was commenced in 1225, and was ready for consecration on 7th July, 1226. It is scarcely likely that in view of the close connection of Tuesday with the Saint's life such an opportunity would be missed.

From time immemorial the 7th July has been the opening day of the local Feast or "Wakes," the Sunday within the octave being "Wakes Sunday."

Many will recollect the Wool Fair which, until the abolition of the local fairs some twenty-five years ago, was held on the 7th July. This fair was undoubtedly referable to the Dedication Festival. As far back as the time of Pope Gregory the Great such gatherings were a "popular and familiar custom and arose from a conflux

---

1. *Historical Memoirs of Canterbury*, John Murray, 1904.
2. All these coincidences are noticed by Stephen Langton, Archbishop of Canterbury, in a tract or sermon circulated by him in the following year to keep up the memory of the Translation.

of people on the Wake,[1] or Dedication Day. Thus," says Burn, "were the anniversaries of a Church's dedication celebrated in populous towns with an accustomed fair and in the most private parishes with feasting and a great concourse of people." He adds that on account of this laudable custom fairs were generally kept in churchyards and even in churches till the indecency and scandal were so great as to want a reformation.

Although there is no evidence that the fairs were ever held in this Church there is proof that they were held in close proximity to it. The Survey of the Lichfield Chapter Estates taken in 1650 mentions a little piece of land called " Deans Yard " and half an acre near to the churchyard " where some part of faire hath used to be kept having on it an old stone house valued at 40/s per annum." It is sad to have to explode a myth current even in the present year of grace that " the Danes fought " in the " Danes Yard," as we now call it,[2] but there can be no reasonable doubt that the present Barn still standing on the South of the Churchyard is the site of the Dean and Chapter's Tithe Barn, and the half acre clearly corresponds with the area of ground now occupied by houses and gardens on the East side of Church Brow between the Churchyard and Burbage House. The wording of the Report just quoted " hath used to be kept " suggests that fairs had ceased to be held there before 1650, perhaps because, as Burn points out, happened in other places " the Puritans began to exclaim

---

1. An old manuscript legend of St. John the Baptist quoted in Burn's *Ecclesiastical Law*, first published in the reign of George II, says the Wake is the customary festival for the dedication of the Church. " In the beginning of Holy Church it was so that the people came to the Church with candles burning, and would *wake* and come with lights towards night to the Church in their devotions: and after they fell to lechery and songs and dances, harping and piping, and also to gluttony and sin, and so turned the holiness to cursedness, wherefore the holy fathers ordained the people to leave waking and to fast till even. But it is still called *vigil* that is *waking* in English.

2. The Derbyshire vernacular would naturally convert " Dean " into " Dane."

against it as a remnant of popery." It is, however, the fact that within the last century wool was still pitched in a croft below the Dean's Yard Barn, called in old documents the Dock Yard or Wool Croft. The late Mr. John Lowe (Joiner) told the writer many years ago that he remembered this being done on Wool Fair Day, and there is still amongst us at least one old parishioner who remembers the Wool Fair as a time of Hiring Servants. Young men paid 2d. each for standing in the Churchyard where the public footpath now is, whilst the young women stood in the Market Place between the Roebuck and Swan Inns and paid 1d. each, hence the spot was known as " Penny Hill."

The Dedication festival was not the only Great Feast of the Church marked in Chapel by Fair Days, for an important Fair was also held on the Thursday before Easter and another on Ascension Day, others being held on Old Michaelmas and Old Martinmas Days. The rents of various building plots leased by the parochial officials were usually reserved payable on " the morrow of Holy Thursday." In the early days of the nineteenth century, and we know not how long before, the Churchyard was a place for the collection of Rates on Sundays. There was an old green gate at the corner leading into Horse Croft Lane and people from over Courses and that side of the parish entered by it. John Fox and " Old Adam Fox of Martinside " sat, one at this gate and one at the Church door, to collect the Church Rate and Poor Rate as the people came to Church on Sundays. All these facts point to the Parish Church being the " hub " of ancient Chapel. Mr. Henry Kirke believes the " Bull's Head " to be the site of the oldest Inn in the town, and although no reference to it can be traced in the eighteenth century Churchwardens' accounts or in Dr. Clegg's Diary, it probably is the old Church Inn. In it may still be seen a quaint rack for storing the old clay pipes known as " Churchwardens."

Opposite to the Bull's Head may be traced the remains of the old Market House *rebuilt* by Mr. John Shallcross in 1700, and behind the Inn, facing the old Fair Ground, was an old building used as a gaol or lock-up. Both of these were in use in the recollection of people not long since passed away.

The writer would like to believe that one of these occupied the site of the still more ancient " Toll Booth," or toll-house,[1] which was in 1405 provided with a new key at a cost of 2d.

---

[1] cf. Wycliffe's Bible "a man sitting in a tolbothe Matheu by name." Authorised Version " at the receipt of Custom." Matt. ix., 9.

The chancel in 1890, before restoration, from a contemporary photograph.

CHAPTER II.

THE CHURCH OF ST. THOMAS A BECKET.

THE CHAPEL-EN-LE-FRITH.

THE Church now consists of a Nave with north and south Aisles and south porch, Chancel and Tower at the west end.

The length of the Nave from the Chancel Arch to the west wall is 56 feet, the width, including the aisles, being 54 feet 4 inches. The Chancel is 39 feet in length by 19 feet 8 inches wide.

It has come down to us traditionally that the present Chancel not only stands on the site of the Chapel of St. Thomas of Canterbury, but that its walls are actually part of the original structure, and on the whole there are good grounds of support for this story.

In 1889, when the roof and walls were in a practically ruinous condition, several independent examinations were made, and the conclusions then arrived at point to the antiquity of the building and to the evidences of its erection in the Early English period. As the reports of these examinations contain the most trustworthy accounts we can obtain of the Chancel as it existed before the restoration of 1890-3 we have summarised them as follows :—

The north and south walls were found to be composed of small irregular stones, the mortar generally being completely gone to dust.

Mr. A. Hill, the builder, who eventually carried out the work of rebuilding the Chancel and restoring the whole Church, draws attention to the thirteenth century style of the Chancel as shown by the string courses under the window sills, some of the jambs of the windows, the internal arrangement and the general character of the work, also to the original height of the roof which was probably of a steep pitch with a single truss, but the exact height of the roof was not then very apparent. With the exception of a piece over the east window the roof was of oak. It was of an exceedingly flat pitch, having probably been made to agree with the nave roof when the latter was re-roofed. The lead on the roof was much worn and had evidently been repaired from time to time. On it was found the inscription "John Byron Minister/ Nicholas Kirk/ Cornelius Pickford/ Church-wardens 1750." It had a battlemented parapet on the south side only, beneath which was a much weathered gargoyle.

The interior walls were covered with plaster, beneath which was found in places a dado of fresco paintings divided into square panels and filled in with rude scroll paintings to a height of five feet from the floor level.[1] Unfortunately these mural paintings, if any existed, could not be preserved when the plaster was removed. A piscina, however, was found in the accustomed place on the south side of the Sanctuary. It is without ornamentation, the upper part being in the form of the drop arch of the Early English period. The fact that this piscina was found in the position it occupies suggests that it is in its original place. During the restoration, however, a "foundation wall" was discovered 9 feet west of and parallel to the present east wall. It is described as being built on stones arranged like old field drains. It is not recorded that this wall was traced beyond the north and south confines of the present chancel, but it would enclose the Priest's door referred to below, and

---

1. This bears out the statement made to us by an old lady that her brother (Dr. R. Bennet) had seen in places in the Chancel where the plaster had fallen away a rude painting which he described as resembling a chariot.

if it were the original east wall of the Chapel, the latter must have been lengthened at some period by 9 feet. The piscina, therefore, may not now be in its original position.

We are enabled by the kindness of the late Mrs. Butler of Burrfields (a grand-daughter of Mr. William Barber, organist for practically half a century) to reproduce from a painting in her possession the very interesting view of the Church forming our frontispiece.[1] A comparison with the woodcut in Glover's *History of Derbyshire* shows that this was taken from our picture with the omission of the figures in the foreground. The painting proves that the outside of the Chancel was plastered prior to 1833 (the date of Glover's work) and also that the window at the south-east of the Chancel was in the position it still occupies. The gable of the tithe barn may be seen in the right-hand corner of the picture.

The removal of the plaster from the stone within and without revealed the stonework of the ancient entrance or Priest's Doorway to the Chancel from the south, the opening being 6 ft. 6 ins. in height and 4 ft. 6 ins. in width inside. Portions of this doorway appeared to be coeval with the ancient structure, mixed however with modern rubble work. The walls generally seemed to have been patched and rough cast at various times either for repair or for blocking up old windows.

To the east of the modern doorway is the window shown in the frontispiece. It is square-headed with three pointed headed narrow lights with plain sunk spandrils between. Opposite to this on the north side is a similar window. Two modern windows of perpendicular type are set on the north-west and south-west sides of the

---

1. The painter was John Taylor, born at Spark Bottom in this parish in 1805, and the picture was probably painted when he was about 25 years of age. He became J.P. for Derbyshire, and was a well-known land agent and surveyor residing at New Mills. He was a member of an old local family still represented at Chapel and Buxton.

Chancel, but there is no trace of the windows they replaced. The Vicar (Rev. J. C. Stredder, M.A.) has kindly lent us the accompanying view of the Chancel as it appeared in 1890 immediately before the rebuilding. It will be noticed that the window above referred to does not appear to correspond, as to position, with Mr. Taylor's picture.

An examination of the footings of the piers in the nave indicated that the nave floor (in consequence no doubt of many burials) was in 1890 and still is some thirteen inches higher than originally, probably there was a single step at the entrance to the chancel so that the floor of the nave would be about a foot lower than the original floor of the chancel which, judging from the height of the piscena as it existed when these examinations were made, would be about its then level. A visitor on behalf of the Society for the Preservation of Ancient Buildings considers the Chancel to be of late rectilinear or Tudor character and describes the East window as a " dreadful restoration." Mr. Alfred Darbyshire, F.I.B.A., of Manchester, says : " What remains of the Chancel is Perpendicular Gothic on the site of the old Church. The present features, with the exception of the piscina or credence arch, are of the worst and most debased period of Perpendicular Gothic."[1]

The old oak altar rails now in the Baptistery were in 1889 *in situ*.

The reports we have quoted point to an original early English structure so far as the Chancel is concerned and that its walls or shell standing in 1889 were part of the old Chapel more or less " restored " at some time during the Perpendicular period and probably altered by the addition or blocking up of windows from time to time.

---

1. The foregoing is taken from reports made to the Vicar and Churchwardens by Mr. Alfred Hill, builder, of Tideswell, Mr. Clifton Wittenbury, of Manchester, and Mr. Darbyshire, also from a report, for a copy of which we have to thank the S.P.A.B.

THE CHURCH OF ST. THOMAS A BECKET 13

The lowering of the pitch of the original roof may have taken place in the latter part of the sixteenth century to agree with the roof of the nave—which bears the date 1599.

The Chancel was practically rebuilt in 1890-3, a considerable portion of the walls being taken down where necessary and rebuilt, all the old material being re-used where possible and the ancient architectural and other features being reproduced, the outline of the old south door, which may be observed within the Chancel, being retained.

A new roof was put on and new tracery in keeping with the rest of the window replaces the former debased filling-in of the upper portion of the east window. New pews or stalls were (at the cost of Mr. Samuel Needham of Lower Eaves) placed in the Chancel facing north and south in place of the previous pews which all faced the west. At this time also an organ chamber was built at the east end of the south aisle, a window being removed and the wall cut through to form an archway which is filled in by an open oak screen.

That the Nave is of much later date than the Chapel of 1225 is not open to question. The arches are built of a warm free stone closely resembling that still worked at Crist Quarry, Bugsworth within Chapel parish, and the Nave is connected with the Chancel by a fine arch of date contemporaneous with the arcades, which are of gritstone.

The north and south aisles are separated from the Nave by four arches supported by octagon pillars. The nave arcades and the caps of the piers and also the respond corbels at the west end are of the Lancet or Decorated period, and date the Church as probably erected in the late fourteenth century.

Professor A. C. Dickie, of Victoria University, Manchester, who has visited the Church and kindly given us the benefit of his valuable opinion, says: " On the evidence of the details the date of the nave arcades cannot be earlier than 1350, and there is every probability that they are later. The detail is too decadent for the middle of the fourteenth century, and it looks much more like a later copy by unskilled craftsmen such as you would expect to find at the building of such a church. There are many examples throughout the region of details being used long after the time when they had been superseded elsewhere. Under the circumstances I feel that the nave arcades might have been built at any time within a hundred years onwards from the middle of the fourteenth century." Professor Dickie adds that Mr. Hennings, an authority on local Gothic work, agrees in this view.

Rickman, in his well-known work on Gothic Architecture, refers to such cases: " There is another pier in buildings which appear to be of this style, which is at times very confusing, as the same kind of pier seems to be used in small churches even to a very late date. This is the very plain multangular (generally octagonal) pier with a plain capital of a few very simple mouldings and with a plain sloped arch. Piers of this description are very frequent, and it requires great nicety of observation and discrimination to refer them to their proper date."

The arches terminate at the west end with responds having corbels each carved in the form of a head. The masonry of the west wall is somewhat puzzling, there being indications of a false wall which is not now quite explicable. The old building line is obvious, marking the pitch of an ancient roof much lower than the present one and having a steep slope. The west wall does not join the belfry arch and is padded on both sides of it with masonry of apparently differing workmanship. A possible explanation of this is that the wall was so built in to strengthen the tower when the latter was built.

On the north side are four clerestory windows of very early style, the jambs being deeply splayed. Corresponding windows were at some period on the south side, but have been blocked up, and there are now only three clerestory windows on that side, of much more modern style than those on the north.

The removal of the plaster ceiling in 1890 disclosed a roof of somewhat barn-like character. The main beams were, with one exception, in good condition and estimated by the builders to be about three hundred years old. These remain *in situ,* wall plates and new carved brackets of oak being provided where necessary. In only one instance was an original wall-plate observed, the beams resting directly on the walls. The beam over the Chancel Arch was much decayed and was replaced. It was found to contain a number of pellets from a shot-gun. This is said to be not unusual, at any rate in this district, the shots being from the gun of some minister or parish clerk who sought to dislodge the birds nesting in the rafters !

The beams are bolted with wooden " throughs " similar in style to those to be found in mediæval barns and other buildings.

On the tie beam at the east end of the nave is deeply incised in Old English characters " H. L. 1599—A.O.," probably the initials of the then Churchwardens, and on the same beam " T. T." is more roughly cut, which is surmised to be a carpenter's or builder's mark. Below the king post on this beam is a carved boss in the form of a wheel-shaped medallion, probably conventional, but which might possibly be intended for the Tudor Rose. It has, however, been ruthlessly damaged to make room for one of the ceiling rafters.

The north aisle has been added after the nave or else entirely rebuilt at some phase of restoration, and windows abnormal to the original date inserted. Of this rebuilding we have no record, but it can perhaps be dated from two inscriptions on the rafters of the roof of this aisle. On one of the principal rafters is " Caleb Cook

Minister Jno Shallcross Thos. Bagshaw Churchwardens 1712."[1] On another rafter at the west end is "Ja. Pickford Clarke Jno. Bennett workman 1712."

This aisle was formerly known as St. Nicholas Quire or Bowden Quire, and at the east end was the seat[2] and tomb of the ancient family of Bowden of Bowden Hall. The tomb, shown in the 1702 plan at the end of the volume, was briefly noted by Bassano in 1710 as a "low raised alibaster stone for Nicholas Bowden of Bowden." It was in existence when Reynolds visited the Church in 1760, and it is much to be regretted that this, the only ancient monument in the church, was subsequently swept away—probably during the re-pewing of 1834. It was not, however, noticed by Rawlins, who was here about 1820. Reynolds[3] says : " Upon an escutcheon in this church are 4 coats quarterly.

1st also quarterly sa. and or, the first quarter charg'd with a Lion passant argent for Bowden of Bowden Hall.

2nd. *Ar.* a chevron bet. 3 crosses fichée *gu.*[4]

3rd. *Ar.* a Lion rampant sable.

4th. Same as first.

Over this achievement is a shield of arms cut in Alabaster for Bowden only, and over the arms a crest which I think is a Hawk's or Eagle's head erased.[5]

There is also a chest tomb of marble near the same (being towards the N.E. corner) but no inscription, neither does there ever seem to have been any as the said shield of arms is large and covers above half the tomb, and the rest thereof is quite smooth and plain. This

---

1. John Shallcross, Esq., of Shallcross Hall and the Old Hall in the Market Place (now the Roebuck Inn), rebuilt the Market House in 1700, High Sheriff of Derbyshire 1710. Thomas Bagshaw, Esq., J.P., of Ridge Hall, gave land at Alstonelee and Crossings Road for the augmentation of the benefice in 1719.
2. See pp. 124, 127.
3. Add. MSS. 28, 111, Mitchell's MS.
4. 2nd Woodroffe of Hope. 3rd Barnby of Barnby. See p. 124 .
5. An eagle's head erased, the crest of Bowden.

church of Chapel-en-le-Frith is also called Bowden Chapel, and in the N.E. corner has formerly been a Chantry."[1]

Two sections of an alabaster slab on which some slender outline of coats of arms may be descried, now in the south porch, are believed to have been portions of the tomb seen by Reynolds. He also noted a small brass plate affixed to the north wall not far from the west end commemorating Anthony Bealott to which we shall refer later.

Reference is found in a list of seat lays made in 1728[2] to "Lady's Quire South Side," and from the placing of graves and seats it seems pretty clear that the position of this chapel or altar must have been at the east end of the south aisle. All trace of this and of the original south aisle has long since vanished in the "restoration" of 1733, and whatever windows existed at that date have been replaced.

The tower, south porch and south side are all of the Georgian Period. Over the porch is a sun-dial dated 1733, and inscribed—

"Ut umbra sic vita."

Dr. Cox remarks that "the architect has attempted to engraft a barbarous classic style with urn-capped parapets upon the ground plan and general structure of a Gothic edifice," and makes some strong remarks on appreciations of the building by Rhodes and Glover.[3] His somewhat sweeping judgment, however, is not confirmed by later authorities who have pronounced the Georgian work to be of bold character and excellent detail, and this is particularly true of the great archway under the tower formerly closed up by an unsightly gallery and the organ, but now opened out—the base of

---
1. We have met with no reference to any chantry connected with the Church. Reynolds had perhaps heard something of Our Lady's Quire.
2. See p. 126.
3. *Churches of Derbyshire*, Vol. 2, p. 146.

the tower being converted into a Baptistery. The effect of the imposition of the Classic on the Gothic style must be admitted to be incongruous, but after all it cannot be derided as a sham restoration in the earlier style. But the masons of 1733 in many cases set the wall stones off their bed thereby reducing a good deal of the work to a grievous state.

The quaint drawing of Chapel-en-le-Frith and its church which is here reproduced from a late Elizabethan plan of the Peak Forest,[1] represents the church as cruciform in shape with a central tower surmounted by a spire with a south transept having a large circular window. Dr. Cox, who comments on this map,[2] whilst pointing out that its accuracy in a topographical sense must be accepted with some caution, believes this sketch to suggest that the church was larger than it now is, and quotes the case of the fifteen hundred Scottish prisoners as confirming this.[3] He also suggests that the great south window was not produced from the draughtsman's own imagination, and again repeats the statement that the church was rebuilt in the early part of the nineteenth century. With all respect to so great an authority we cannot accept this dictum. A careful comparison of the sketches of other Peak churches in this map shows a certain amount of conventional treatment rather than of accurate representation. It is true that in the early part of the eighteenth century reference is made to the "Steeple" in the Registers, and the present tower is so styled in the building contract, but in Lancashire—and no doubt elsewhere—the term is used to this day quite indiscriminately.

The belfry is still lighted by a large round window on the south side, but again there is no ground for suggest-

---

1. Duchy of Lancaster Maps and Plans, Nos. 7, 37, 34. The parts are numbered separately but are really fragments of one map.
2. *Memorials of old Derbyshire*, pp. 283 et seq.
3. See p. 147.

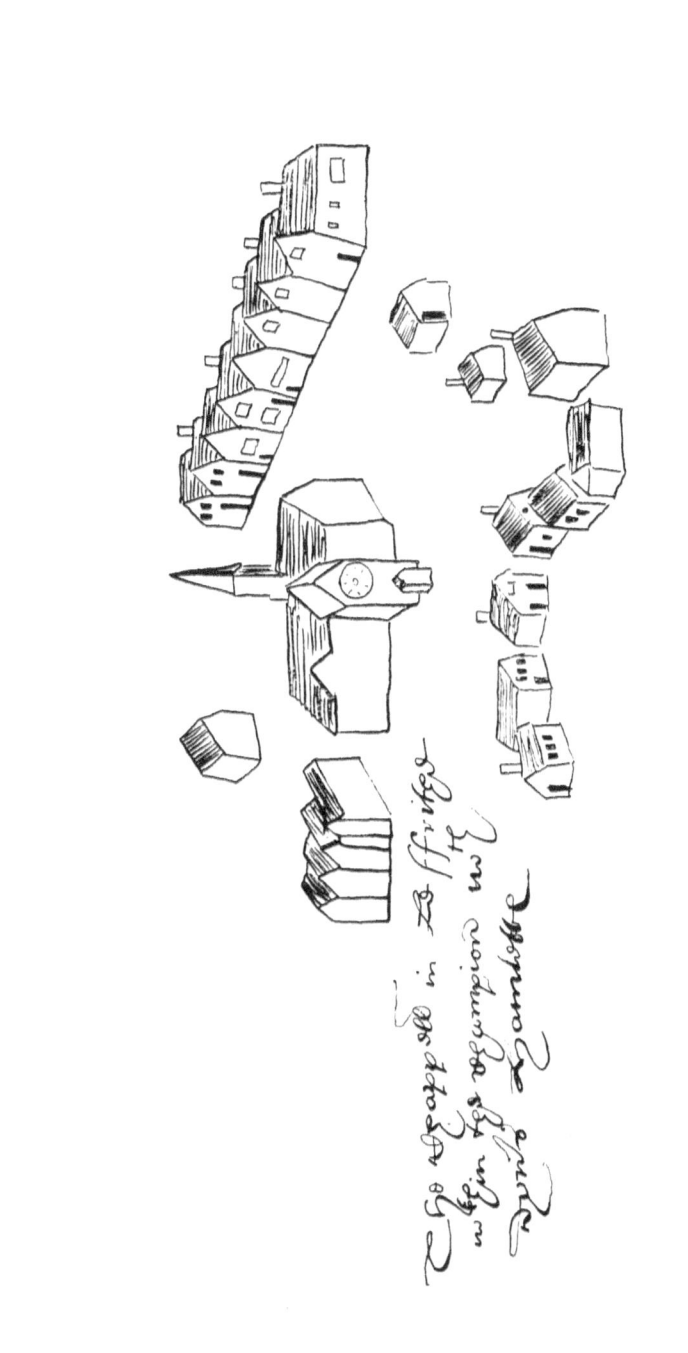

THE CHURCH OF ST. THOMAS A BECKET

ing that it is an imitation of the earlier window, and a glance at the frontispiece shows that this window once held the clock.

What is more puzzling is that the 1709 plan places the steeple at the west end of the north aisle and indicates no south door. This plan is very crude and shows no sign of being drawn to any scale, but its accuracy in such a material point can hardly be doubted. It is to be noticed, however, that a space is left unappropriated corresponding roughly to the approach to the position of the present south porch : we therefore assume that there was a doorway there not shown on the plan.

The configuration of the ground on the north side of the church precludes any suggestion that any part of it could have extended beyond the limits of the present north aisle, moreover, careful enquiry demonstrates that no sign of foundations outside the limits of the present building have been disclosed when opening graves or vaults.

According to the Brief for rebuilding the church in 1731, the steeple had been taken down by the parishioners two years previously to prevent its falling, and the Churchwardens accounts for 1729 show a payment of £10 10s. 0d. for this work to Mr. Platt who afterwards built the present tower.

On the east end of the nave roof is a bell-cote of true Georgian type obviously put there in 1733 to replace an earlier one. It is said that well within living memory there was a bell in this cote which was removed to a house in the parish where it was used as a yard bell. Enquiry corroborates this, and that it fell to pieces some years ago, apparently from old age ! That such a bell existed in this bell-cote and was used for many years for purposes alien to its original function as a Sanctus Bell, no doubt in entire ignorance of its real signification, is an undeniable fact, for traces of the stay for the bell and of the friction of a chain are still visible.

The lead on the roof of the nave and south aisle bears inscriptions recording the eighteenth century repairs. On the nave roof is the date 1733, whilst on that of the south aisle is inscribed " Jasper Frith John Wainwright Churchwardens 1733," and over the south porch " George and Henry Ward 1733." The parapet on the south side of this aisle was also repaired in 1828, partly with brickwork, and in one place a portion of a gravestone, on which the dates May 9, 1758, and Nov. 12, 1760, and the name " Matthew " are still legible, was neatly fitted in.

"OUR LADY'S QUIRE."

There is now no trace or sign of the side Chapel or Altar dedicated to the Blessed Virgin Mary, but there is ample evidence that it existed in pre-Reformation days. We find various references to such a chapel in the first half of the sixteenth century and once subsequently in the Seat Assessment, dated 1728.

John Bennet of Glossop by his Will dated 1534-5 gave " For a stoke to our ladies server of the Chapel of the Frythe,"[1] and in an agreement dated 23rd April, 2 and 3 Philip and Mary (1555) between Agnes Ashton of Chapel Milton and her sons a sum of money is agreed to be paid on Christmas Day and Midsummer Day " between the sun rising and the sun setting upon the Altar of our Blessed Lady in the Chapell en Lee Frithe."

A witness to the Will of Henry Bradshaw of Bradshaw Hall in 1521 was " Sir John Bredbury our Lady prest," who may have served his Altar. Stephen Bagsha, also a witness, is described as curate of Chapel. We can find no other record of this Altar, which apparently was in existence close down to Elizabethan times, whilst its memory was retained for a century and a half later.

---

1. A learned correspondent suggests that stoke = stock or fund, the income of which was to be applied to the upkeep of the Chaplain, no specific sum or article being mentioned.

Interior of the church from S.W.

THE CHURCH OF ST. THOMAS A BECKET

The *Font*, according to the old plan as near the west end of the north aisle, is now in the Baptistery beneath the tower. It is of plain octagon construction and apparently of the fifteenth century. On one side is a shield carved with a quatrefoil. The vicissitudes of this ancient relic are told in another place. During its long absence from the church a small wooden basin with an inside leaden cup was attached to the altar rails and used for many years.

Dividing the Baptistery from the Nave is an oak Jacobean balustrade inscribed " Ex opera guil. White A.M. Anno Domini 1681."[1] This was formerly a portion of the altar rail and was removed to its present position in 1894, but the remainder of the rail has disappeared. The oak panelling in the Baptistery was erected in 1894 " by a number of those baptized in the Font of this Church," as a tablet records.

Dependent from the Nave roof is a fine brass *Chandelier* with wrought iron chain of Flemish character, bearing the inscription " Benjamin Bardsley Minister, John Shirt, Edward White, Churchwardens 1731." This appears to have been acquired at this date but nothing is known of its history prior to 1731. Some reference to this Chandelier will be found in the Chapter on the Churchwardens' accounts.

Previous to the 1894 restoration a tall *Pulpit* stood on the north side of the chancel arch flanked on the south side by an equally tall Reading Desk with a Clerk's desk beneath. The 1702 plan shows the pulpit of that day as adjoining the first pier on the north side, and on this pier and the arcade above can still be seen the plugholes into which the supports of the pulpit and its sounding board were fixed. The present pulpit was the gift of Mr. John Taylor, J.P., and his brothers and sisters[2] in memory of their mother Mrs. Mary Taylor.

---

1. William White was Minister 1670 to 1695.
2. Nephews and nieces of Mr. John Taylor, the painter of the picture from which our frontispiece is taken.

As we have before remarked the church possesses no ancient stained glass or monuments, and, with the exception of the Bowden Tomb, there is no sign that any ever existed.

The east window is about to be filled with a beautiful window representing Our Lord in Glory, the gift of Mr. Ernest Bagshawe, J.P., as a memorial of the seven hundreth anniversary of the church and in memory of the late Mrs. Bagshawe. On the north side of the Chancel is a window of modern perpendicular tracery with fine stained glass, " The Ascension," erected in memory of Norman Bennett, born March 1828, died April 1879, by his widow and sons.

The middle window of the South Aisle is filled with stained glass in memory of the Rev. SAMUEL HENRY PINK, a former Curate and Vicar of the Parish, the subject being " The Good Shepherd."

In the Baptistery beneath the tower is a modern three-light window in Tudor style, " Christ blessing Little Children," to the memory of WILLIAM ARTHUR MILWARD who died 17th March, 1893.

The east window of the north aisle has representations of Faith in the centre with two figures at the side, both apparently typifying Charity, in memory of MARY BENNETT who died 20 July, 1878, and her sister ELIZABETH BENNETT who died 7 Jan., 1879, both of the Stodhart family. This window is, perhaps unconsciously, placed here very appropriately, for it may quite properly be taken to commemorate St. Nicholas whose Quire was situate here.

The centre window of this aisle is filled with stained glass, the subject being " The Raising of Lazarus," in memory of ELIZA, wife of the Rev. JOSEPH LOWE, M.A., Vicar of Haltwistle and Canon of Carlisle, who died 14 Jan., 1897, and of his eldest son, ROBERT BARKER LOWE, who died 1 January, 1881. It is understood that the relatives of Canon Lowe are about to place another window to his memory in this aisle.

The Church contains a number of modern memorials.

In the Chancel. At the east end on either side of the Communion Table are engraved on marble the names of all the men of the parish who fell in the Great War, 1914-18, as follows:—

OUR VALIANT DEAD, 1914—1918.

Appleton, John W.
Baddeley, Edward L.
Bagshawe, Geoffrey H.
Bate, William R.
Belfield, Harry
Bennett, Albert
Boylan, James
Bramwell, Tom
Buckingham, Richard
Cox, John W.
Crompton, J. Barlow
Dakin, Henry
Durkan, James
Evans, Richard
Fletcher, Harry
Fletcher, James
Ford, Clement
Ford, Elisha
Ford, Francis E.
Ford, Harry
Ford, Herbert
Ford, James
Ford, Joseph
Ford, Joseph E.
Ford, Joe
Greatorex, James
Hall, James

Hart, James F.
Heather, Arthur P.
Hoyle, Albert E.
Jackman, H. H.
Jackson, David
Jackson, George L.
Jagger, Harry
Jones, A.
Kelsey, Percy
Lomas, G. W.
Lomas, Jacob
Lomas, Tom
Longson, James
Mellor, John R.
Metcalfe, Charles L.
Metcalfe, Neville
Morten, Erling L.
Muir, Samuel
Mycock, Sam
Nadin, George
Nadin, Victor
Newlands, Jack
Newlands, William
Oldfield, Harry
Peers, James
Pell, Charles R.
Potter, John A.
Potts, Arthur E.
Potts, Frederick

Royle, Harry K.
Ryan, Peter
Saunders, John J.
Shepherd, John J.
Sidebotham, Herbert
Simpson, Arthur
Simpson, G. Harry B.
Simpson, John J.
Simpson, William W.
Smith, Hubert
Spafford, Arthur L.
Spencer, James A. S.
Storer, Sam
Tinsley, Joseph W.
Tomlinson, Frank
Turner, George M.
Turner, Samuel
Williamson, Frank
Walker, Harold H.
Wallis, Alfred B.
Ward, John S.
Waterhouse, George H.
Watts, John W.
Wells, Walter
Yates, Edward

The table itself is of very plain oak. On the front panel is inscribed " Minis^r J. S., E. W., C. W., 1731." Evidently the initials of Mr. Bardsley, the then minister, whose name appears with those of John Shirt and Edward White on the Chandelier in the Nave, have been destroyed at some time when the table has been " patched up," for there is no sign of any further inscription. It is no doubt the table for which Ezekiel Shuttleworth was paid a guinea (see page 97). When Dr. Cox visited the Church half a century ago he noted over the Communion Table " a very inartistic representation of the Last Supper, said to be a copy of an old master." We believe this is now preserved in the chamber over the boys " National School."

South Side. *Marble Monument* to JAMES HEALD of Brinnington, Cheshire, who died 16th May, 1815, aged 58 (a native of this parish), and LUCY his wife, died 26th January, 1844, in her 85th year.

Marble Monument in memory of WILLIAM BENNETT, Solicitor, of Wellclose, who died April 16th, 1879, aged 82, and his wife ERNESTINA MARY, daughter of Colonel Schutz, who died August 25, 1865, aged 64. Marble Medallion portrait of JAMES HEALD, J.P., D.L. (son of James and Lucy Heald), died at Parrs Wood, Didsbury, October 26, 1873.

Marble slab commemorating JOHN JAGGER, who died 14 October, 1911, for twenty years a member of the Choir—erected by his fellow members of the Choir and Bible Class in appreciation of his sterling character and devotion to duty.

Brass plate setting forth that the east window was restored by Norman and Robert Ottiwell Gifford Bennet, A.D. 1876, in memory of their mother Mrs. ERNESTINA MARY BENNETT (referred to above).

Beneath the adjoining window is an inscription that it

was restored by Dr. R. O. G. Bennet, in memory of his wife JESSIE MARIA BENNET, who died 28 October, 1888.

Chancel, North Side. Marble Monument to the Rev. WILLIAM BAGSHAWE, A.M., Vicar of the Parish, December 1790, to November 1792, for 53 years Vicar of Wormhill, who died November, 1847, ANNE, his wife, died 5 November, 1842, and WILLIAM their son, who died 9th November, 1818.

Brass. Rev. JAMES GIVEN, M.A., LL.D., Vicar 1891—1901, died 20th February, 1904.

Marble Monument. Rev. GEORGE HALL, died 15 April, 1885, aged 82, Vicar for nearly 49 years.

Marble Monument in memory of the Rev. SAMUEL GRUNDY, who died Oct., 1836, aged 79, Vicar for 18 years, and MARGARET, his wife, died A.D. 1849, æt. 87.

Brass. ELLEN ELIZABETH, wife of Major Charles Yelverton BALGUY, and daughter of Mr. Henry Marwood Greaves, died 29th December, 1899.

Marble Monument. HENRY MARWOOD GREAVES of Ford Hall and Banner Cross, Esq., died 10 March, 1859, and MARY CATHERINE ANNE, his wife (daughter of William Bagshawe of Ford, Esq.), who died 10 July, 1878.

Brass. MARIE LOUISE, wife of W. M. C. G. BAGSHAWE, who died 20 Oct., 1891.

Marble Plate. In Memory of WILLIAM MURRAY CAULDWELL GREAVES BAGSHAWE, Lieut. Imperial Yeomanry. Lost at Sea off the coast of Madagascar on his return from Active Service in South Africa, 20 May, 1901.

Marble Monument. In memory of HENRY KIRKE of Eaves, died 23 November, 1841.

New stalls are now being placed in the Chancel, the gift of Mr. Ernest Bagshawe, J.P., of Ford Hall, as a memorial to his late wife Mrs. FRANCES ALICE DEVEREUX BAGSHAWE.

South Aisle. Marble Tablet to the memory of THOMAS DAVENPORT GOODMAN of Cromwell House, who died 4 June, 1875. Erected by Sunday School Teachers and Scholars and Officers and Men of 7th Derbyshire Rifle Volunteers and friends.

Tablet to HAROLD HADFIELD WALKER, Acting Segt. 19th Manchester Regiment. Volunteered 8 September, 1914. Died of wounds sustained on the Somme 11th August, 1916. " He loved duty more than he feared death."

Marble Monument to BAGSHAWE family of Ford Hall.

Tablet to TOM BRAMWELL, 6 Batt. Sherwood Foresters, killed in Action at Kemmel, Belgium, May 19th, 1915. Sexton of this Church. " A workman that needeth not to be ashamed."—2 Tim. xi. 15.

Marble Monument to the memory of WILLIAM HENRY GREAVES BAGSHAWE, Esq., J.P., D.L., of Ford Hall and Banner Cross, died 12 July, 1913.

West End, over South Door. Hatchment of Queen Anne, Royal Arms and " A. R." (This was formerly over the Chancel Arch in the Nave.)

On West Wall a *Brass Tablet* inscribed :—

" The Bells of this Church were rehung at the sole expense of the late Mrs. Eliza Slack of Bowden Hall, in this Parish in the year 1885, and the Nave Windows were renewed at the joint cost of Mrs. Slack and other Parishioners in 1886; the remaining portion of the Edifice being thoroughly repaired and restored in 1891-5, by the undermentioned Trustees of the late Samuel Needham, Esq., of Rushop in this Parish, who bequeathed £2,000 for the purpose; the Organ Chamber was provided in 1893 at the expense of his nephew, Samuel Needham,

Esq., of Lower Eaves, the Organ being at the same time enlarged and improved by the Parishioners and others, and the West Gallery was removed in 1897 also at the cost of Mr. Needham of Lower Eaves.

J. Given, M.A., LL.D., Vicar.
Joseph Heathcott, Churchwarden 1884 to 96.
James C. Hyde, Churchwarden 1886 to 98.
J. B. Boycott, Churchwarden 1896 to 98."

Stone Slab. " Domine Refugium
DAVENPORT GOODMAN ELIZABETH his wife
KATHARINE EATON and ELLEN their daughters
1806   1920."

Marble Slab. To THORNHILL family 1798—1844. " N.B.—There are six breadths of graves belonging to this family betwixt the North wall and the pulpit pillar."

Slate Slab. ELIZABETH, Wife of Wm. BRADBURY of White Knowle in Chinley, died Sep. 1, 1803, aged 71 years.

North Aisle, East End.

Monumental Marble to PETER BOOTH, died August 20, 1844, and was for upwards of thirty years a faithful and diligent medical practitioner in this parish and MARY his attached wife, died 17 March, 1844.

Stone Slab in memory of SAMUEL NEEDHAM of Lower Eaves who died Dec. 18, 1919. "The memory of the Just is blessed."

North Wall. Monumental Marble in memory of Mrs. CATHERINE BAGSHAW (widow of Samuel Bagshaw, Esq., of Ford), died Apl. 10, 1828.

Monumental Marble to the memory of the said SAMUEL BAGSHAW, Esq., D.L., who died 16th May, 1804.

When Reynolds visited the Church he noted here a

Brass Plate which has now vanished, inscribed: " Near this place lieth the body of ANTHONY BEALOTT,[1] Yeoman, who married Susannah the daughter of Stephen Staly, Gent, by whom he had five sons and two daughters. She died Nov. ye 5th, 1661, aged 42 years, and he died May 20th, 1702, aged 84 years.

Given by Joseph Bealott the 3rd son, now living in Leverpoole."

At the west end of the north aisle is a *Stone Coffin* removed into the Church from the Churchyard wall some thirty years ago. The Stone is similar to that used in building the Nave. Reynolds on his visit to Chapel May 1, 1760, saw this coffin and says: " On ye right hand as you enter the Churchyard is a stone coffin placed upon the top of the wall (instead of coping) in the bottom

---

1. The family of Bealott or Bellot were for many centuries settled in Combs Edge, where their estates are still held by their descendants, the Jacksons. Another representative is Mr. H. L. L. Bellot, a well-known legal writer.

of which, near the middle, is a round hole about four inches in diameter. This coffin is about 6 ft. long within. There is another stone coffin like this at the sign of the Thorn Tree in the towne with a hole in the middle like the above-mentioned, which said last-mentioned coffin serves for a watering trough, being placed under the Pump, and has the said Hole occasionally stopped up with a plug. Whence these were is not now known but they have been villainously carried out of the church when the fabrick was built some 30 or 40 years ago." A sketch of this old coffin is here shown.

The " Thorn Tree " in Market Street has long ceased to be an Inn and no trace of this coffin can now be found.

The Churchyard.

The original Churchyard must have been of small dimensions and, as was usual with ancient churches, the greater part lay on the south side.

It is not unlikely that the half acre or so below the road where " some part of fair hath used to be held " was once open to the Churchyard, although it may not have been used for the purpose of burial. The old Churchyard may be identified by the lines of trees—some planted in 1756 and some in 1762, which still flourish. Since the latter date there have been three additions, the last and largest being made in 1903, when about an acre and a half of land on the north side of the then existing graveyard was purchased and fenced in by public subscription.

The most noticeable feature is, perhaps, the number of burials of non-parishioners to which we allude in the account of the old custom of burial within the Church.

In some parts of the older portions of the Churchyard it may be observed that the inhabitants of separate hamlets rest together in neighbourly fashion as they did in life.

The ravages of time and of the "tempestuous and ill weather" of which we, like our ancestors, still complain have entirely obliterated the inscriptions on many a headstone, the oldest now legible that we have been able to find being two close together, at a little distance from the east end of the Chancel marked

1631   and   1634
A. L.   John Lingard.

The P. R. tells us that Anthony Lingard of Chapel Milton was buried on 20 June, 1631, and "John son of George Lingard of the Milton being a scholler" was buried on 22 April, 1634. The map of 1709 shows a number of graves in this vicinity dedicated to various branches of the Lingard family.

On the south-east side of the Chancel is a small curiously shaped stone, probably the oldest inscribed

stone in the Churchyard, on which is rudely carved the representation of an axe, locally termed "the woodman's axe," and above this in more modern characters the initials P. L.. If this was originally a headstone it has probably been appropriated for a later burial.

Another quaint seventeenth century inscription roughly cut on a flat stone, also near to the south-east corner of the Chancel, is as follows:—

"Here lieth/the body of Ellin/the wife of Robert Bennett/of Haugh dau/ghter of Rob/ert Bradbury/of/Bankhead/Gentleman/who departed/this life the /eight day of/October Anno/Dom 1669/and Robert /set this stone/on Ellins grave/this is the/stone of Ellins grave/unto this/day."

The eighteenth century tombstones are usually in good condition and quite legible—one of the earliest of these is that of Thomas Moult, near to the South Porch, dated 1711 and shown on the Map.

Epitaphs and the usual verses are rather conspicuous by their absence, a notable exception being those inscribed on the graves of the Foxes of Martinside, from which we cull the following from the tomb of Adam Fox who died in 1801, aged 73:—

"Farewell vain world I've had enough of thee,
And now I am careless what thou sayst of me,
Thy smiles I court not nor thy frowns I fear,
My hopes in Christ although my dust is here."

Near the south wall of the Church in the midst of a colony of namesakes lies a learned son of Chapel thus commemorated:—

"Here rests the body of/Thomas Hallam/a member of the Council of the/English Dialect

Society/ Born 26 December 1819/ at Raglow[1] Chapel en le Frith/Died 7th September 1895/at Ardwick Manchester/ He devoted the leisure moments/of a long and busy life/to a patient and diligent enquiry/into all that is noteworthy/in the various dialects/of Northern England/ The results of his Studies are/placed in Bodley's Library/in the University of Oxford/.

Past to where beyond/these voices there is peace."

Near to the main entrance is a circular walled enclosure bearing the names cut in stone of DANIEL WOOLEY and ROBERT OLERENSHAW, Churchwardens in 1737, and ROBERT HIBBERSON and JOHN LOMAS, wardens in 1760. A story still current is that this was the site of a cockpit, but another and more probable one is that it was used to enclose an old yew tree the last relics of which disappeared seventy or eighty years ago.

Near to the south porch is a column on which is a metal sun-dial, this column being of a pinkish free-stone similar to that used in the Nave of the Church and bearing a strong resemblance to some of the crosses still to be seen in some parts of the Peak Forest. An examination of some old houses on the west side of the Churchyard, now having entrances to Church Lane, suggests that these old dwellings at one time had their frontages to the Churchyard. One of these, as we have recorded elsewhere, was, in the early eighteenth century, the home of the incumbent. Either by burials or, more likely, by the deposit of débris from the old spire, the levels have been considerably altered and the doorways and windows partially blocked up.

---

1. This should be Draglow. Mr. Hallam bequeathed a valuable collection of books and dictionaries to the Library of the Chapel-en-le-Frith Institute.

GIFTS TO THE CHURCH AND ITS MINISTERS.

We have already referred to the bequest by JOHN BENNET of Glossop by his will dated 5 Jan., 1534-5, of a "Stoke to our ladies server of the Chapel of the frythe," and mention below the gift of £20 by the will of FRANCIS GASKELL, dated 16 June, 1718, the interest to be paid yearly to an orthodox minister at Chapel, which was invested in the building of the Old Parsonage, the owner of which property pays £1 per annum to the Vicar.

WILLIAM BARBER, of Malcalf, by his will dated 4 February, 1666, left one-third of his estate to be disposed of as counsel should think meet for pious and charitable uses for Chapel-en-le-Frith, some account of which Charity is given in Chapter XII.

THOMAS MARSHALL, of Combs, by his will dated 8 August, 1708, gave the sum of £100, the interest to be paid yearly as to one half to the minister in priest's orders in Chapel-en-le-Frith and the other half for apprenticing a poor child of Combs Edge. This sum was laid out towards building the central portion of the west gallery, the pew-rents arising from which were divided between the Vicar and the Overseers of the Poor until the gallery was removed in 1894, when the late Mr. Needham of Lower Eaves gave £100 to replace the original sum.

ELIZABETH SCHOLES, by her will dated 5 October, 1734, directed that £52 10s. 0d. should be put out and the interest paid to the Churchwardens of Chapel and laid out in buying twelve manchets or loaves weekly to be distributed every Sunday immediately after morning service in the Church, to such poor housekeepers and poor children as should attend that service, as the Churchwardens should think proper objects. The Report of the Charity Commissioners in 1835 says at that time the Churchwardens provided six twopenny loaves on 50 Sundays in the course of the year which they distributed to the poor in the Church.[1] This Charity is now administered by the Parish Council.

A tablet formerly in the Church gave particulars of £20 left by DOROTHY SUITE (or SHIRT) for pious or charitable uses, but all record of this had been lost before 1835.

In the will of NICHOLAS CRESSWELL—of the Blackbrook family—dated 17th April, 1762, is a bequest to the Rev. John Byron and his successors of £20 for a sermon to be preached on the first Sunday after old Candlemas Day " out of and from the 32nd Psalm in the Bible, and the 5th verse," which runs: " I acknowledge my sin unto Thee and mine iniquity I have not hid. I said I will confess my transgressions unto the Lord: and Thou forgavest me the iniquity of my sin ": a curious text to select; perhaps the echo of some tragedy better sunk in oblivion. We cannot find any record of such a sermon being preached—it may be that Mr. Byron knew the reason for the choice of this text and renounced the legacy.

There have been numerous other gifts to the poor and for schools—chiefly by will—but these do not come within our present purview.

We have already noticed the brass plate in the Church recording several modern gifts to the Church and other gifts in our notice of the interior of the Church. The plain Marble Reredos and Brass Altar Rails were the gift of other parishioners in 1894.

---

1. At that date white bread was a luxury to the children of the poor. An old man born at Eccles Fold in 1825 told the writer how as a child he and other children used to look out for people returning from funerals to get a bit of " burying cake," a three-cornered bun, always provided at a funeral at which, if the family were poor, the guests would pay one shilling each towards the expenses. He well remembered the great treat when the " scholars walked " (apparently at Queen Victoria's Coronation), and each had tea and a currant bun. The recollection of the currant bun was much stronger than of the occasion, of which the old gentleman had only a hazy idea.

THE CHURCH PLATE 35

In 1897 Mrs. Bayley of Broughton Park, Manchester, gave a set of Cambridge Chimes for the Church Clock in memory of her parents Henry Constantine Renshaw, Esq., J.P., of Bank Hall, and Lucy his wife. The Chimes ring the quarters cumulatively, the full hour giving music to the verse :—

> "Lord, by Thy Power
> Our footsteps guide,
> So in this Hour
> No foot shall slide."

THE CHURCH PLATE.

The Communion Plate consists of a Pewter Flagon with cover inscribed "John Frith and Henry Ward, Churchwardens, 1736"; also a Paten inscribed "Chapel-en-le-Frith, 1747." This has been "improved" by a stand being added and an etching inserted on the plate itself. There are also two cups bearing no mark : it is stated that the tops of these have been cut and are not in the original state.

Two silver Cups with Paten inscribed "In commemoration of Peace—The Gift of Samuel Needham of Lower Eaves, Chapel-en-le-Frith. Easter Day 1919. J. Clifton Stredder, M.A., Vicar."

In addition to the above the Church possesses a plated Wine-Strainer, presented by Mr. John Bennett, late of Stodhart.

CHAPTER III.

The Men of Bowden and their Chapel.

At present we have no authentic knowledge of the gradual peopling of the Peak Forest and particularly of that part most interesting to us known as Longdendale. We may suppose that during the century and a half following the Norman occupation a fairly steady flow of "immigrants" was taking place—really a species of colonisation. First, royal servants, huntsmen and foresters, their families, adventurers, *bona fide* settlers and perhaps not a few poachers and fugitives from justice, and following all these a sprinkling of artificers and tradesmen. Local place names suggest the presence of dwellers in Saxon times, and the Danish system of grouping two or three homesteads together for mutual defence and companionship is very marked. We must not, however, place too much reliance on place names as evidence of earlier occupation, for the language and customs of most of the early settlers would be more akin to the Saxon than to the Norman type, and if the younger Peverel's grant to Lenton is to be accepted this part of Langdendale was mainly waste in 1150. We are, however, not concerned at the moment so much as to whence or how the population came as with the fact that in the first quarter of the thirteenth century the district of Bowden was fairly inhabited. Dr. Cox (*Churches of Derbyshire*, vol. ii, p. 139) states that "the foresters and keepers of the deer became so numerous that about 1225 they purchased a portion of the Crown land held by William de Ferrars and built themselves a chapel for Divine Worship which they called the Chapel in the Forest (frith)."

Dr. Cox does not give his authority for the statement

that the land was "purchased," but he no doubt derived it from the records to which we shall now refer. William de Ferrers, grandson of Robert de Ferrers, the first Earl of Derby, was Bailiff or Custos of the Peak, *i.e.*, the chief local authority, from 1216 to 1222. Robert de Ferrars, the son-in-law of the last Peverel, had been permitted to hold certain of the Peverel lands, although the Peak Forest does not appear to have been included in these. His grandson, however, took the opportunity of King John's wars with the Barons to make himself heir of all the Peverel estates without due royal warrant, and had confirmed Peverel's grant to the Priory of Lenton. This naturally caused the Priory to lay claim to the Advowson of this new chapel and to two parts of the great tithes and all the small tithes pertaining to the cultivated land springing up round about it. The Dean and Chapter of Lichfield, on the other hand, claimed the tithes as the possessors of the Advowson of the Church of Hope in which parish, they asserted, the new chapel was situated. At pleas held at Derby in 1241,[1] these rival bodies were called upon to show cause why *the King* should not present a suitable "parson" to Chapel-en-le-Frith then vacant.

It is thus clear that almost immediately after its foundation the question of the patronage of the Church became a live one.

In answer to the claims of the Priory and the Dean and Chapter Adam de Eston on behalf of the King contended that William de Ferrers had thrust himself into the position of heir to William Peverel when the war was raging, and neither he nor the Dean and Chapter had obtained any Royal Warrant for the new Chapel and as to the claim of the Priory, the site was waste when Peverel made his grant. This roll is unfortunately

---

1. Abbrev. Placet. 25 Hen. III. Rot. 25. Cox II. *Churches of Derbyshire*, p. 140.

incomplete, but it was decided that if either party could produce any Charter or confirmation from the King it should not be set aside.

After the proceedings at Derby in 1241 no records have survived until we find an *Inquisition ad quod damnum*[1] held at Fairfield on Monday after the Feast of St. Luke, 11 Edward II (24 Oct., 1317), when the foresters, verderers, keepers and freemen to the number of upwards of forty, sworn and charged upon their oath in the premises made the following statement as to the Chapel of Frith. We set out the original in order that the reader may have the exact wording which is somewhat peculiar :—

Dicunt eciam quod dominus Henricus Rex avus Regis nunc approiavit se de quadam villa que vocatur Boudone in qua plures sunt Hameletty Et quod post approiamentum huiuismodo factum quedam capella fundata fuit in solo predicti Regis Henrici per homines tunc temporis habitantes Et vocatur Capella del Frithe Et postea per quendem Episcopum Conventriensem et Licheffeldensem Alexandrum nomine concessa fuerunt eidem Capelle Sepultura et Baptistarium tempore eiusdem Regis Et modo est Ecclesia parochialis Et quod Decanus et Capitulus Licheffeldensis et Prior de Lentone et conventus eiusdem Ecclesiam illam tenent in proprios usus de qua advocacione se habeant verum Titulum an non ignorant.

This may be translated :—

"They say also that the lord King Henry Grandfather of the present King had for his own profit a certain *vill*[2] called Boudone in which are many hamlets and that after such appropriation a certain Chapel was

---

1. 11 Edward II. No. 97.
2. *Vill.* here appears to mean a district, as there was no town at that time, and "Bowden," strictly speaking, included not only the area subsequently called Bowden Chapel, but also Bowden Middlecale, the whole of the latter being in Longdendale.

THE MEN OF BOWDEN AND THEIR CHAPEL 39

founded on the soil of the said King Henry by the men then inhabitants and called the Chapel of Frith and afterwards by a certain Bishop of Coventry and Lichfield Alexander by name were conceded to the same Chapel Burial and Baptism in the time of the same King and now (*modo*) it is a parish church and that the Dean and Chapter of Lichfield and the Prior of Lenton and the Convent of the same hold that church to their own use of which advowson if they have a true title or not they (the deponents) are ignorant."

Amongst these deponents several appear to be connected with Chapel-en-le-Frith, *e.g.*, Thomas, son of Thomas le Ragged, Richard Brown (possibly of The Marsh), two Foljambes, William Hally and Nicholas Baggeshage (foresters), Robert del Cloghe, Benedict de Shakelcros (regarders), William on le Kerkyard and Nicholas de la Forde.

It will be noticed that the deponents say the chapel was founded on the King's soil which seems to confirm Adam de Eston's contention that no Royal Warrant was obtained, but they may have been speaking in the sense of the feudal theory that all land was held of the King. Be that as it may, we venture to suggest that behind the desire, no doubt quite sincere, for the spiritual facilities this chapel would afford, there was on the part of the Forest Officials, another and important social and economic intention. The records that have come to light in recent years show that by the beginning of the thirteenth century a considerable population was springing up in the Forest, particularly in Longdendale along the valley of the Goyt : within a few miles was the Royal Hunting Box, " Camera Regia in Foresta Pecci," still commemorated by the Farm known as " The Chamber," and surrounded by an area, now the Parish of Peak Forest but then extra parochial, enjoying until recent years peculiar civil and ecclesiastical jurisdiction.

Our suggestion then is that this Chapel was placed in Bowden for the express purpose of attracting to its precincts a community who were to found a new town which should be, as it has always claimed and still claims to be—the Capital of the Peak. This is no mere parochial boast. Let us look at the facts.

It is perhaps not generally recognised that in the twelfth and thirteenth centuries the foundation of new towns was carried out in England as well as on the Continent of Europe on political and economic lines on quite a large scale. At the very time of the erection of our church the new city of Salisbury was being laid out on a scientific town-planning system, and three Altars in its Cathedral were consecrated in 1225—Liverpool had just been founded by King John, but not on systematic lines. Later, in 1281, Edward I laid out the town of New Winchelsea and ordered his Commissioners to assess certain " burgages " or building sites and let them for buildings at fixed rents.

Through the valley in which Chapel lies runs, from east to west, the ancient way to which we have referred, which can still be traced from Sheffield—Salter Lane— through the Hope Valley and over Mam Tor to Eccles Pike and Bowstone Gate as a direct road from South Yorkshire into Cheshire. At the " town end " of Chapel this road intersects another, probably of equal antiquity, passing roughly north and south, giving access to Lancashire, North Cheshire and West Yorkshire on the one hand, and on the other leading by way of Ashbourne Lane[1] to Tideswell and to the Roman Road at Batham

---

1. The late Mr. R. Holland of Ashbourne derived the name of that town from the British *Ash* = water, and Saxon *Bourne* = a stream, an interesting example of a compound word in two languages having a similar meaning—in this case lit. a water lane. To this day a fairly strong stream flows alongside the road, and in old times probably ran over it. Drovers have told the writer that they took cattle by this way from Chapel Town end to Monyash in practically a straight line. It may also be observed that this road, which passes close to the " Bull Ring " at Dove Holes, follows very nearly the " sighting line " from Arbor Low to Chinley Churn.

Gate and further on to the South and West Midlands. Several other ancient ways that need not be specified converge on the Chapel valley from all sides, and on a slight elevation in the vale stands the Church—a landmark from practically every point of approach. North and east of the Church lie lands known for generations as Burrfields, said, we cannot say with what absolute authority, to be a corruption of *Boroughfields, i.e.,* the Common fields of the Burgesses, adjoining to which fields and close to the Church is Dane's (or Dean's) Yard, which is undoubtedly the site of the tithe barn, and is bounded on the south by the ancient way. The position was, therefore, admirably adapted for the site of a new town. In the Forest Pleas for the time of William de Horsedon, Bailiff (*c.* 1250), we find " in the vill of Chapel-en-le-Frith " a number of Burgages and half Burgages[1] held by, amongst others, William Capella, Elias de Marchenton, Robert de Marchenton, Matilde de Thorneley and others.[2] We are not aware that Burgage tenure is recorded as existing in any other part of the High Peak. There is evidence that the area of the " Borough," as it is often called in old documents, approximately extended from School Croft adjoining Cromwell House to Ashbourne Lane, and from Burrfields to the Brook below the present Cricket Ground. The owners of Borough lands were entitled to set up stalls in the Market Place, for which they paid small rents only, and the profits were divided amongst them on the Morrow of Holy Thursday: they were exempt from all offices except that of Headborough. They

---

1. In some parts of Wales a burgage was a plot of 80 by 60 feet, in others 40 by 60 feet. Jacob's Law Dictionary defines a burgage as "an ancient tenure proper to Boroughs whereby the inhabitants by custom held their lands and tenements of the King or other Lord of the borough at a certain rent. It is a kind of socage tenure and signifies the service whereby the borough is holden. Anciently, a dwellinghouse in a borough town was called a Burgage." Jacob adds, "*Borough* is sometimes used for *villa insignior*, a country town of more than ordinary note not walled."

2. Yeatman, *Feudal History of Derbyshire*, sec. vi., p. 294.

appear to have acted by the Parochial officials or by some of their number by the title of "the Burgesses of the Borough of Chapel en le Frith" as late as the second half of the eighteenth century, and in many old deeds dwelling houses in this area are described as "burgages." We need not remind our readers that the Courts Leet and Swainmote Courts of the Manor of High Peak were held here as are their successors, the County and Magisterial Courts, to this day, and the town is still the Parliamentary centre of the High Peak Division. Another illustration of the importance attached by ecclesiastical authority to this "Chapel of ease" lies in the fact that Bishop Stavenby at once granted rights of baptism and burial to it.

Whether the Church were founded for the purposes we have indicated or merely as a Chapel of ease to meet the wants of a growing population the date of its erection can be clearly established. Alexander de Stavenby was consecrated Bishop of Coventry and Lichfield at Rome in the year 1224 and died in 1238. As it was he who gave the building rights of baptism and burial, which he could do as the owner of the advowson of the Mother Church of Hope—apart from his power as Bishop—it follows that it must have been built between these dates, and there is no evidence to controvert the statement of Dr. Cox ascribing the foundation to "about 1225." It is known that this Bishop formally ordained the vicarage of Hope, and it is fair to assume that the boundaries of the present parish of Chapel-en-le-Frith were fixed at the same time, and that if not constituted a parish church the new building had parochial rights in a defined area. These boundaries were carefully set out, for in several places the limits of division follow no obvious natural limit, as, for instance, the straight line drawn across Combs Moss from a point on the Old Road above White Hall to Durrans Low separating Chapel-en-le-Frith from what became the Township of Fernilee, which for more than six centuries remained part of the Parish of Hope, and the similar arbitrary line on Colbourne Moor dividing Chapel from Castleton Parish.

At that period these divisions could be made with the more ease because large tracts adjoining to, and both within and without the parish, were in the hands of the Crown as part of the "Wastes" of the Forest. The very artificial boundary between Chapel and Fernilee suggests the possibility that at first the latter township was intended to form part of the new parish. Both were at one time in the parish of Hope or in the area of the ancient church of Hope, which eventually became that parish. In Peverel's grant Shallcross and Fernilee are mentioned, but there is no reference to Bowden which, having then no distinct entity and being separated by no natural boundaries, may have been included with Shallcross and Fernilee as part of the "pastures." That Chapel-en-le-Frith, or Bowden Chapel, as it is often called, and Fernilee must have been closely connected is shown by the fact that down to 1842 the "curate" of Chapel received one-third of the tithes of corn and hay arising from Fernilee, and it is also on record that rent-charges from land in the same township were made payable at the south porch of the Church of Chapel-en-le-Frith. But in the case of Fernilee down to the recent formation of the Ecclesiastical parish it had no separate rights of baptism or burial as against the Mother Church of Hope. The title of the new Church, Capella del Frith,[1] shows it to have been primarily erected as a

---

[1]. The earliest reference to "Chapel-en-le-Frith" that we have seen is in 1241. We are not here concerned with the etymology of the word "frith," which has been the subject of so much learned discussion, but although we personally incline to its meaning a "forest" rather than a "clearing" we must confess that the theory we have propounded as to the reason for the erection of the Chapel tends to support the latter interpretation. In considering this question it must, however, be borne in mind that at this time less than half the parish was "cleared," as is proved by the Forest pleas and the Awards made when the final disafforestation took place in the seventeenth century, and if the town was intended to be the capital of the Peak the word "frith" may well be worthy of the wider interpretation.

Chapel of Ease to some Mother Church, and such Mother Church could only be that of Hope. It is true that for many generations the minister or incumbent was called cappellanus, the usual designation of a perpetual curate, but as Burn (*Ecclesiastical Law*) tells us "cappellanus vicars or curates all meant the same office," and a perpetual curacy of ancient foundation has been legally distinguished from a mere ancient Chapelry by its possession of parochial rights, *e.g.*, of baptism and burial and the rights of the incumbent to small tithes and surplice fees. That it had a separate advowson certainly appears to have been suggested as early as in 1241, and at the Inquest at Fairfield in 1317, it was declared that Bishop Stavenby conferred the rights of baptism and burial, which confirmation cannot have taken place later than 1238, "and it is now a parish Church."

Some light is thrown on the status of Chapels of Ease and their Chaplains by that great ecclesiologist Cardinal Gasquet.[1] Public Chaplains, he says, were those who served in Chapels of Ease, "such Chapels were *built at the cost of the people of the parish and under careful restrictions laid down by the Bishop of the diocese.*" An instance is given in the case of a Chapel of Ease at Dartmouth in 1372 where the people living there—in the Parish of Townstall (which was a vicarage, the benefice being appropriated to the Abbey of Torre)—built a chapel without the consent of the Abbey or Vicar. After some difficulty Bishop Brantyngham of Exeter dedicated the chapel and allowed a baptistery and cemetery, and the people were allowed to find a chaplain to serve it who was to be licensed from year to year and admitted by the Vicar of Townstall. This case bears a certain analogy to our own and may be useful when we come to consider the claim of the parishioners to present to the benefice.

---

1. *Parish Life in Mediæval England*, pp. 99, 100.

THE MEN OF BOWDEN AND THEIR CHAPEL 45

As showing the importance of Bishop Stavenby's grant of baptism and burial it must be borne in mind that rights of a mere chapel of ease to baptism and burial may be concurrent with the parish Church, and this was so in at least one instance within Hope parish. The evidence as to Chapel-en-le-Frith all points to these rights being granted and enjoyed exclusively and not concurrently, and there is nothing to indicate that the persons inhabiting the area which became by ordination or custom assigned as a parish to St. Thomas à Becket's ever had any rights or duties in respect of the Mother Church or its incumbent. It is also clear that the Chaplain took the small tithes and surplice fees. The Vicar of Hope took the Easter offerings at Fernilee, but there is no instance of his doing so at Chapel.

Until the year 1300 in all trials of the right of particular churches, if it could be proved that any chapel had a custom for free baptism and burial such place was adjudged to be a parochial chapel, and hence at the first ordination of these chapels care was always taken in the ordination of them, if they were to continue in subjection to the Mother Church, that there should be no allowance of font or bells.[1] Mr. Cresswell in his petition[2] expressly lays stress on the fact that Chapel Church does possess a font, bells and other attributes of a parish church.

The Parliamentary Commissioners of 1650 say this place is a parish and donative,[3] the latter statement no doubt being made owing to their misunderstanding the Dean and Chapter's peculiar jurisdiction. In the same year the Survey of the Chapter Estates reported that the right of presentation and donation " is the parishioners (as they affirm) and hath been so beyond all memory of man : The manner of election is thus, Twenty-seven of

---

1. Phillimore's *Ecclesiastical Law*, 2nd ed., p. 1454.
2. See p. 62.
3. A donative is a preferment in the free gift of the patron without presentation to or instituture or induction by the bishop.

the chief of the inhabitants or the major part of them choose their minister and the rest are all to subscribe by ancient custom which they still observe." This was only partly correct as is explained in Chapter V. The twenty-seven were an advisory Committee only, but this fact must have been forgotten or overlooked within thirty years of their appointment. The Incumbent, for some hundreds of years styled Cappellanus, Chaplain, Curate and Minister, is now under the Statute 31 and 32 Victoria ch. 117, styled Vicar and the Benefice is officially recognised as a Vicarage.

The right of Advowson, *i.e.*, to present or nominate a Clerk in Holy Orders to a vacant benefice, possessed by the inhabitants, ratepayers, or vestry of a particular parish, although unusual, is not so uncommon as is popularly supposed.

In the case of Chapel-en-le-Frith the right is now clearly established, but how it came to be acquired must in great measure remain a matter of conjecture.

The early history of the Church of Hope and of the Tithes of the High Peak may throw some light on the subject, but it is to be feared that the actual history of the advowson must continue a mystery in the absence of documentary evidence.

After careful consideration of the available facts it is suggested that an explanation may be as follows:—

By the grants of John, Earl of Mortaigne, to the Bishop of Coventry and Lichfield, followed by subsequent grants and confirmations by later Bishops to the Dean and Chapter of Lichfield, that Body became the Parsons or Rectors and would—in the absence of other factors—have the patronage or advowson of daughter Churches in the parish—hence *prima facie* the advowson of the Chapel-en-le-Frith would be theirs. This is borne out by the allegations of the witnesses in 1618 of the liability of the Chapter to repair the Chancel for which the Rector is usually liable, although in the present instance the Chapter do not seem to have troubled very much about this duty. There were, however, several other factors in the case. In 1241 the Priory of Lenton claimed the advowson under the grant of two-thirds of the tithes of Hope Parish by Peverel: the Crown also claimed it on the ground that the Chapel had been built on the King's soil without royal warrant to either Peverel or the Dean and Chapter,[1] and on land not within the grant to the Priory as being waste at the date of that grant, and the Dean and Chapter claimed it as the proprietors of the Mother Church.

The decision in this litigation—if a decision were arrived at—unfortunately being lost we can only assume from after events that whilst, as between the parties, the Priory retained the greater part of the tithes the Chapter held the advowson.

The foresters and others who testified at the inquest *ad quod damnum* in 1317 say the Chapter *and* Priory hold the advowson to their own use, but profess not to know by what title. They do not suggest that it was in the freeholders or parishioners, or that the inhabitants had any right or privilege of nomination.

Some thirty years later, in 1350, Queen Philippa (then Lord of the Castle and honour of the High Peak) nominated Thomas del Clough (a local name) unto the Chaplaincy of Chapel-en-le-Frith "annexed to the Church of Hope," and the Chapter issued their Commission to one of their Canons to aid in repelling the intruder.

The only known instance of an attempt to nominate in right of the Priory occurred after the dissolution of the Priory by the Countess of Shrewsbury,

---

1. This somewhat controverts the argument on p. 40, but regal memory is sometimes short, and the foundation of the Church and "Borough" may have been carried out without obtaining the immediate sanction of the Crown.

whose sole claim in that right could be as owning the Priory property then vested in the Cavendish family, and even then she appears to have been acting in conjunction with the Dean and Chapter.

A possible explanation lies in the fact that the Dean and Chapter had by prescription a "peculiar jurisdiction" with regard to several Derbyshire Churches, including Hope and Chapel, under which jurisdiction they had the power to make institutions and inductions without the confirmation and approval of the Bishop of the Diocese.

The Church is described in the *Valor Ecclesiasticus* of 1535 as a *capella* not as an *ecclesia*, and it is given in Ecton's *Theasaurus* (1754) and Bacon's *Liber Regis* (1786) in a list of Chapels belonging to Bakewell. This is clearly an error as nothing connecting the Chapel with Bakewell is to be found elsewhere.

By virtue of the acts of Bishop Stavenby the Chapel immediately upon its consecration obtained certain parochial rights. The analogy of the Dartmouth Church case to which reference has already been made can now be applied.

There the people who had built their Church (as the men of Bowden are said to have done) were allowed to find a Chaplain to serve it who was to be admitted by the Vicar of the Mother Church of Townstall—a secular clergyman, the benefice being appropriated to the Abbey of Torre. The Chaplain in this instance was to serve for a year, but this, certainly after the middle of the fifteenth century, was not so at Chapel. If "finding" the chaplain means providing his stipend as well as nominating him the people of Chapel must have had this duty thrust upon them as in 1650, and for a century later, their Chaplain had not more than £8 allowed him by the Dean and Chapter "and no other income beyond the people's gratuity."

In this connection the phraseology used in the cause

of *Thornhill* v. *Tooker* may be significant. Cresswell alleges that the custom was for the people to *present* and for the Dean and Chapter to *accept and admit* the Chaplain, and Mr. Bowden deposes that on such presentation the nominee had been *allowed and inducted*.

The probability therefore is, that whilst, as one of the questions put to the witnesses suggests, the Dean and Chapter had (in right of their " peculiar ") exercised episcopal jurisdiction in the parish and, notwithstanding that the parsonage was appropriate to them, they had, as in the Dartmouth case, permitted the people to make the nomination in consideration of their providing the greater part of the Chaplain's stipend.

With regard to the status of the Church the most reasonable view seems to be that, whilst by the concession of rights of baptism and burial the Church became possessed of parochial attributes, yet by accident or design it was never duly constituted a parish Church, but, whether it were so constituted or not, ecclesiastical authorities and inhabitants alike have for centuries tacitly accepted it as a Parish Church. As a learned correspondent whom we have consulted points out, many parishes were never formally constituted—they just grew. The language of the deponents at the Inquest in 1317 leaves little doubt that by the use of the material word " *modo* " in its mediæval sense of " now " they intended to affirm the fact of actual parochiality at that time. It is noticeable that in the Chapter's Receipt Roll for 1339, Robert de Sydebotham is described as " of the parish of Chapel en le Frith," but this perhaps can be claimed only as evidence of the assumption we suggest rather than of the fact, and the same may be said of Edward Cresswell's assertion in 1617 that the Church has a font, etc., " and other parochial attributes," whilst the petition of the churchwardens and inhabitants alleges that there has been from time whereof the memory of man is not to the contrary " an ancient parish church or chapel."

We are, however, inclined to think that Cresswell and his supporters did intend to imply a parish.

The Ecclesiastical Commissioners now recognise Chapel-en-le-Frith as a parish and not a mere parochial chapelry or perpetual curacy.

After the foundation of the Church comes a long silence broken only by the Inquest of 1317—our knowledge of the Church's history during the next two or three centuries being but such as we may meagrely gather from its stones—and of the people who built the Nave, the descendants and successors of the " men then inhabitants," the builders of the original Chapel, we know practically nothing. Surnames had not really come into use in the Peak in 1225, and such names as we find at first recorded relate chiefly to places or occupations. William Kirkyard or William at the Churchyard may, and probably did, later develop in Kirke, and so on. We have noticed the names of the earliest holders of " burgages " and of some of those who gave evidence at Fairfield. Later in the thirteenth and following centuries we meet in Forest Court Rolls and old Deeds and Duchy of Lancaster Rent Rolls other names, some now lost, but many still represented.

In 1322 we find in documents relating to lands in Chapel the names of Bagshaw, Ollerenshaw and Horderon; in 1345 a witness to a grant of land in Bagshaw to one William Boles is Robert Mould. Kirke and Bradshaw and Brown and Bowden are amongst the earlier names, and during the fourteenth and fifteenth centuries we find Bellot, Bramhall (Bramwell), Ashton, Greensmith, Gibb, Lumhales (? Lomas), Mellor, Taylor and Thornhill to mention only a few patronymics repeated again and again in the Parish Registers and list of officers.

This, however, is not a history of the Parish and space does not allow us to enlarge on this interesting theme.

CHAPTER IV.

THE TITHES OF THE PEAK FOREST AND THE CHAPLAINS' INCOME.

TITHES AND EASTER OFFERINGS.

To seriously discuss the question of the Tithes of Chapel-en-le-Frith in relation to the very small fraction thereof received by the Minister may almost appear to be an attempt at a bad joke. Nevertheless the question is of interest as being wrapped up in the larger issue of the right of presentation.

In their inception Tithes were a levy or payment of the tenth part of all a man's possessions for the maintenance of the Bishops and Clergy and are of much more ancient origin in England than the Parochial system itself. In return, the Bishops and Clergy had certain duties—clearly defined as time went on—with regard to the application of the Tithes they received. We shall see how the Tithe-owners of the Peak interpreted that duty—and their methods were common throughout the country.

We have mentioned that Peverel granted two-thirds of the tithes of the Peak and other places to the Priory of Lenton. Burn in his *Ecclesiastical Law* tells us that the custom of the Early Church to divide the tithes into three parts, one of which was allocated to the parish priest for his own immediate occasions, led to lay patrons disposing of the other two-thirds to other pious uses which conduced to many gifts to Monastic bodies, as in the present case. When the Church of Hope was passed by the gift of John of Mortaigne, first to the Bishops and then to the Dean and Chapter of Lichfield the latter as

"Rectors" naturally claimed the tithes not disposed of by Peverel's gift. This was the position in 1241 when the long struggle began between the Capitular authorities and the Priory which, with brief intervals of peace was only terminated by the suppression of the Monasteries under Henry VIII. The history of this litigation does not immediately concern us and those interested will find full details in Volume V of the Derbyshire Archæological Society's Journal.[1] The importance of the controversy is demonstrated by the fact that during the three centuries of its continuance there were five several appeals to the Papal Court at Rome.

Very scandalous scenes took place at Tideswell in 1250 and 1251 reflecting grave discredit on the representatives of these so-called religious bodies.

On one occasion the Dean's men having collected a number of tithe sheep and lambs in the district actually folded them in Tideswell Church (an older one than the present fabric) when the Prior's servants broke in "some sheep and lambs were killed under the feet of the horses in the Church: others were dragged out and carried off by force of arms: the Ministers of the Church were beaten and savagely wounded and the Church itself violated by the Ministers and Monks of the said Prior and Convent and polluted with blood and the Churchyard likewise."

Happily no such occurrences are recorded as disgracing this parish.

Amongst the Chapter documents is a roll recording two Inquisitions taken on oath in 1251 with remarks, and intended for the use of the Proctors engaged in the litigation. It gives details of the events we have just described and particulars of the tithes claimed by the Dean and Chapter.

Under the heading of the Parish of Hope is the

---

1. To which we are indebted for these particulars.

TITHES AND EASTER OFFERING

following: "The Prior and Convent possess two parts of the Great and Small Tenths in the hamlet (*villula*) del Frith and certain other hamlets adjacent thereto, namely Ford, Malcave, Whithalge, Bradshaw, Lightbirches, Tunstead, Combs, Greater Horderne, Bagshaw, Little Blackbrook, Whitehills, Lesser Horderne, Brede (? modern Broadlee), Ollerenshaw, Thorneylee, Heylee, and Alstonlee which are called Forest land and the Great tithes are worth 14 marks, but the Small tithes 7 marks. In these places W. Peverel never cultivated the said lands in his own name or another's."

The last statement—if correct—shows that in 1150 the district must have been "pasture" as Peverel describes it, and that most or all of the hamlets mentioned were founded after that date and affords further evidence of the comparatively rapid growth of the population immediately prior to or after the building of the Church. One of the questions in dispute in the litigation was as to whether Peverel had the right of bequeathing tithes of land not under cultivation in his lifetime.

Another important point to be noted is that this document refers to these Hamlets as still in the Parish of Hope nearly a quarter of a century after Chapel Church was built and may lend colour to the view that Chapel-en-le-Frith was then but a parochial chapelry. About this time a temporary peace was patched up by which the Priory took two-thirds of the Great Tithes of the pastures and places then cultivated in, amongst other places, Chapel-en-le-Frith. The litigation need not be further pursued, but we may remark that this division was roughly followed until the Tithes were finally commuted.

In 1272 the Chapter Registers say the Priory was entitled to £20 6s. 0d. from Chapel and 11s. from Shallcross and Fernilee, the former sum being much larger than the figures for any of the adjoining parishes, but a survey of the Alien Priories taken 3 Richard II

(1380) assigns £4 only of the tithes of the Parish of "Capella del Frythe" to Lenton.

It may be convenient here to refer to the state of the tithes in 1842 when they were commuted under the Tithe Commutation Act 1837. At that time the tithes were and had been for centuries paid by way of *modus,* a fixed customary sum, instead of in kind, as follows:—

Great Tithes. A *modus* of £12 in lieu of Corn and Hay of which the Duke of Devonshire[1] took two-thirds, *i.e.,* £8, and the Curate (Incumbent) one-third, *i.e.,* £4. This was payable in respect of about 5,300 acres, it being then stated by Mr. Thomas Gisborne, M.P., that the remaining 3,800 acres never paid these tithes, being originally a Royal Chase, and this was no doubt correct, for by prescription no tithe was paid for agistment or ley of cattle. From this we learn that when the division of the Wastes between the King and the tenants was made in the time of Charles I, about one-third of the parish was waste or common land, *i.e.,* was not prior to that time disafforested.

Small Tithes. Tithes of wool and lambs (part of the Small tithes) were payable in respect of *all* lands in the parish, and of these the Duke of Devonshire was entitled to two-thirds and the Dean and Chapter of Lichfield to one-third. The Curate was entitled to all the other small tithes and to the customary Easter offerings. The following customary payments were made in lieu of the Curate's part of the small tithes : 1½d. for every milch cow and calf, 1d. for every barren cow, 1½d. for every mare and foal, 1d. for each hen and duck, 1½d. for each pullet, 2d. for each turkey and goose, 1d. for every hive of bees and 2/6 for each litter of pigs.

Comparing these payments with those in Chinley we find that within that Township the Incumbent was

---

1. Representing the Priory of Lenton.

entitled for every turkey, duck or hen to two eggs at Easter " sending one to gather them," and he was also entitled to " a plough penny, a hay penny and a garden penny," and each chimney 1/2d. " for smoke," and every tradesman " for his hand 1d," as an Easter offering. These payments do not appear at Chapel or Fernilee and only a plough penny was gathered at the Mother Church of Hope.

The Easter offerings at Chapel were 3d. for a man and his wife, 1½d. for a widow or widower, and 1d. for each unmarried person above 16 years of age. Individuals were less valuable in Chinley, married couples paying 2d., while all others were exempt.

It is curious to notice that at this time the *modus* of £1 for Corn and Hay in Fernilee was divided in the same proportions as at Chapel between the Duke of Devonshire and the Curate of Chapel, the latter receiving 6/8d. The *modus* for Small Tithes and the Easter offerings were received by the Vicar of Hope, but were exactly the same in both parishes. These facts again suggest a close connection between Chapel and Fernilee and are further evidences that the two were originally in Hope parish. It was pointed out at the time of the commutation that certain rent charges were made payable in the south porch of the Parish Church of Chapel-en-le-Frith.[1] It would indeed appear not unlikely that for a time at least Fernilee was ecclesiastically joined to Chapel.

On the final Commutation of the Tithes the Dean and Chapter took £6 13s. 4d. per annum as their share of the Wool and Lamb Tithes, on which basis the whole of these tithes would be worth £20 a year. The Duke of Devonshire allowed his share of the Great and Small

---

1. In a Shallcross Deed of 16 Edw. III. (1341) the annual acknowledgment is a pair of white gloves at the Feast of the Translation of St. Thomas the Martyr, the Patron Saint not of Hope but of Chapel.

Tithes to be extinguished, and the Curate accepted an annual rent charge of £4 per annum for his share of the Great Tithes and £10 in respect of his share of the Small Tithes and Easter offerings. Certain waste land of the parish on Colbourne Moor and another plot still known as Poors Piece were at this time conveyed to the Rev. Wm. Bagshawe of Ford in consideration of which he agreed to pay this sum of £14 per annum to the Incumment of the parish, and this is now paid by the owner of a Farm called "White Lea" near Rushop, on which the payment is charged.

Having thus shortly considered the history of the tithes we see how that history has affected the Chaplain's income and has reacted throughout the centuries on the claim to the Advowson of the Church.

The lion's share went to the Priory and through it passed to the Earls and Dukes of Devonshire.

On the dissolution of the Monasteries the possessions of the Priory of Lenton were confiscated and granted by the Crown to Sir Francis Leech. About this time one Sir William Cavendish, a member of an old East Anglian family, was high in favour with the Sovereign, it is said through the influence of Cardinal Wolsey, and was employed in the suppression of the Religious Houses. For these services he was rewarded by the grant of valuable Abbey Lands in Hertfordshire and elsewhere. He afterwards exchanged these for other late monastic possessions in Derbyshire and Nottinghamshire, and purchasing Chatsworth he married the famous Bess of Hardwick and became the founder of two ducal houses, Devonshire and Newcastle. It is obviously under this title that his widow, then Countess of Shrewsbury, endeavoured to interfere in the presentation to the Living and "the most part of the parishioners" of Chapel are almost the only people who can claim to have successfully thwarted her during her long and eventful life.

Mortuaries.

At an early period it was the custom for a man to leave to his parish church at his death a gift as a set off against any personal tithes or offerings that he had not duly paid in his lifetime.[1] In impropriated parishes such as Chapel, this became diverted from the parish church and its incumbent and went, in the Peak, to the Dean and Chapter of Lichfield. The Lord of the Manor claimed as a " heriot " the " best good " either horses, cattle or household furniture.[2] The Church then came in and claimed the " second best," but, as we said, the vicar for whom it was originally intended did not get it. A roll for the year 1339 was discovered by Dr. Cox,[3] from which we extract some items relating to Chapel. It gives some idea of values at that date, always recollecting that money had then at least fifteen times its pre-war value. A beast was only taken if the deceased had three, so that if a man had a horse, a cow and a calf, the lord took the horse, the Church took the cow and the surviving relatives kept the calf : each item commences " For the body of."

For the body of Margery del Ford of Chapel one worn tunic which is given for the Love of God.

Dyonisius, son of Hugh of Bagshaw, the half (*medietatem*) of one ox sold for 4/-.

William, son of Hugh del Clough, 1 ox sold to William of Wheston chaplain for 11/- settled for 9s. 8d.

Robert de Sydbotham of Bonges in the parish of Chapel del Fryth 1 bullock sold to Peter Gyfford for 4/-.

Richard en le Lane of Chapel 1 cow sold to Richard of Hatton for 7/-.

---

1. cf. The Will of Joan Brocklehurst, p. 122.
2. We have a case in mind at Hope where the Lord made this claim within the present century, and compounded it for a money payment.
3. *Derbys. Arch. Socy's. Jour.*, xi., p. 150.

Alice, wife of Richard de Horderne, 1 ox sold to John le Porter for 12/-.
Richard Douche " de capella " 1 cow sold to Peter Giffard for 6/-.
Richard de Hirdefeld de Capella 1 ox sold to Gervase Vicar of Baucquell for 14/-.

In the Capitular Records is a fragmentary list of payers of Wool tithe in the parish for the year 1491 giving the number of tithe fleeces of wool.[1] The names appear to be those of residents in the Combs Edge district and are as follows:—

Thomas (?) Coker, Ux. Robt. Crossley, Nicholas Brown, Henry Bagshaw, Thomas Bramall, Thomas Cowp(er), Wm. Belot, Richard Cowp., Thomas Aleyne, Thomas ffernle, Walter Melor, Ux. Edward Aleyne, Rico. Redferne, Ada Redferne, ux. Nichs Yown, Ux. Willi Redfern, Thomas Marlar, John Redferne, Robert Redferne, Hochor Cowp., Robert Mellor, Radi Ollerenshaw, and Robert Ollerenshaw. The total number of tithe fleeces is 112.

Other names (most of them connected with the Bagshaw and Ford side of the parish) are Nichs. Cresswell, Lawrence Greensmith, John Cresswell, Margaret Greensmith, Ux. Hugh Gibbe, Thurston Dicson, Ux. William Greensmith and John Hobson. These appear to have paid no tithe.

The Chaplain's Stipend.

How the Ministers existed during the first five centuries of the Church's history remains somewhat of a mystery. The Dean and Chapter took all the tithes they could secure from the hands of the Priory of Lenton and also received the Mortuaries. It would seem that in the sixteenth century all the income of the Chaplain was

---

1. Communicated by Mr. Edward G. Bagshawe.

THE CHAPLAIN'S STIPEND

about £8 a year from the Dean and Chapter and such surplice fees and Easter offerings as he could gather. It is rather a matter for surprise that the benefice could be filled at all, and we can only look upon the case of this parish as another instance of the devotion of the mediæval (and modern) country clergy, of the bulk of whom it may be said, like the parson who made the famous pilgrimage to the Shrine of our patron Saint:—

" Christe's lore and His Apostles twelve
He taught, but first he followed it himselve."

As we have suggested in another section, the short stay in the parish of many of the Ministers is quite intelligible when we remember that well into the eighteenth century the incumbent could not even claim to be "passing rich on forty pounds a year," but if the eulogies on Mr. Bardsley and the second Mr. Byron are to be trusted they, at least, were animated by a very different spirit from that of their contemporary

" Who thinks his Sunday task
As much as God or man can fairly ask."

Perhaps in the early days the Chaplain made a little profit out of the leases of the tithes and Altar dues which were granted from time to time by the Dean and Chapter, as witness a lease to Thomas Armitage, Chaplain in 1534, of the tithes of Corn and Hay at Chapel for five years at a rent of £8 payable to the Chapter's Attorney at the Church at Tideswell.

In 1650 the Survey of the Chapter Estates says that £4 6s. 8d. is paid to the Minister, and adds "there is no other means belonging to the minister except the people's gratuity." In this same year, however, the Parliamentary Commissioners report that it is worth £10 13s. 4d. If the larger sum is correct it can hardly be deemed excessive.

When, in the last years of the seventeenth century, the

Rev. Wm. White became "disordered in his mind" and incapable of performing the Duty, the Churchwardens agreed to allow him 4/- a week for his life and to provide another Minister as curate, the whole income of the living then being about £16 or £17 per annum. It was said at the time that an Order of Sessions was obtained, probably under the Poor Law, and it is not surprising to learn that during Mr. White's indisposition " the Church was but very indifferently supplied."

Down to this time and for twenty years after there was certainly no glebe land attached to the benefice, and there is no reference to any official residence for the Minister.

In a Settlement made in 1716 by John Middleton of Wirksworth, Mercer, a son of Robert Middleton of Chapel, Mercer (a great friend of Dr. Clegg's and the writer of several quaint notes in the Parish Book) there is mention of a dwelling house in Chapel wherein Caleb Cooke, Clerk, then dwelt. The house contained a " foreroom or dwelling house, the buttery then in two parts, with a washhouse and chamber over it and the little shop in the town street and a garden." The Middletons owned several houses adjoining Church Lane and some land below. There is an old house or part of one in Church Lane on the south-west side of the Churchyard which still shows signs of some pretention, and moreover has an ancient doorway, now blocked up, into the Churchyard which answers the above description, and we suggest that this was the residence of Mr. Cook and probably of some of his predecessors.

Mr. Cook died in August, 1717, and was succeeded by the Rev. John Byron. Soon after the latter's induction the parishioners took up the question of providing a permanent Parsonage and in January, 1722, Arnold Kirk, Ralph Gee and seven others purchased a plot of land adjoining Back Lane from Thomas Shuttleworth. This purchase was made on behalf of several freeholders and others who had subscribed to build a house for the Minister and his successors. Kirk and Gee were the Trustees of a sum of £100 left by Francis Gaskell (of the Bank Hall family) in 1718 from the income of which 20/- per annum was to be paid to an orthodox Minister at Chapel-en-le-Frith, and they gave £20 to the building fund on condition that the house should be charged with the payment of £1 a year to the Minister for ever. One hundred and twenty years later, the Rev. George Hall purchased a plot of land, then part of the King's Arms Croft on the east side of the Old Parsonage, as it is still called, and so enlarged the garden. The Old Parsonage was occupied as the Vicarage House until 1849 when Mr. Henry Marwood Greaves and his wife (*née* Bagshawe of Ford Hall) gave the site of the present Vicarage House and garden: the Old Parsonage was sold and the proceeds of sale with donations and a grant from Queen Anne's Bounty, were expended on the present Vicarage. The owners of the Old Parsonage still continue to pay £1 per annum to the Vicar.

In 1719 Mr. Thomas Bagshawe of the Ridge, in consideration of £200 paid by the Governors of Queen Anne's Bounty, conveyed to them lands valued at £400, comprising a farm at Alstonelee and two fields in Crossings Road, once part of Roeside Farm, as an augmentation of the Living, and subsequently other lands in Chapel and Chinley were purchased with the aid of grants from the Bounty. With the exception of the Crossings Road land and a small quarry in Chinley these lands have been sold to advantage and the proceeds invested.

The present gross income of the Benefice, according to the Southwell Diocesan Kalendar, is £270, with a Vicarage House.

CHAPTER V.

THE PARISHIONERS' RIGHT OF PRESENTATION.

IN whatever manner the right of the parishioners to nominate or present a Minister was acquired, it is clear that this right was exercised—although it may have been under protest—at the early part of the sixteenth century and was then recognised as being firmly established. This is apparent from the depositions in the action of *Thornhill and Gibbe* v. *Tooker* taken at Chapel on 25th March, 1618.

In or about the early part of the year 1617, Francis Barney, the then Minister, desiring to resign, attempted to procure the preferment by the Dean (Dr. William Tooker) and Chapter of Lichfield of his brother Thomas Barney to the vacant benefice in his place. The parishioners, however, standing on their ancient customary rights, elected one Edward Cresswell, B.A., " a learned religious and reverend preacher," whom the Chapter refused to accept. Mr. Cresswell's parentage is unknown, but if he were a member of the local Cresswell family we can understand that the personal element would embitter the struggle against this refusal to acknowledge a cherished right.

Cresswell, himself or by his friends, at once took up the quarrel and petitioned the Chapter. A rough and very dilapidated draft of this petition—in parts torn and in other parts illegible—is happily still preserved in the Church safe. The document, partly in English and partly in Latin, runs in essence as follows:—

> In the Name of God Amen. To the Venerable and Exalted (*egregius*) men in the Lord the Dean and

THE RIGHT OF PRESENTATION 63

Chapter of the Cathedral Church of Lichfield and their Deputy or other competent Judge or Judges in that behalf on the part of the worthy and discrete man Edward Cresswell against Thomas Barney of the Parish of Chapel en le Frith, Clerk, and others before you in judicial proceedings it is alleged as follows:

1. Anciently, there was and now is in the town of Chapel a certain Church or Chapel consecrated having a baptismal font a table for the administration of the Divine Sacraments a belfry bells a cemetery for the burial of the dead and other parochial attributes.[1]

2. That in time back the said Church or Chapel with its rights and appurtenances was annexed and impropriate by the Dean and Chapter to their own use.

Clauses 3, 4 and 5 are much mutilated, but so far as legible set out that from ancient times it had been the custom for the Dean and Chapter to appoint a Curate to perform Divine Service in the said Church and that for " 200, 300 or 400 years past " it had been the custom for the dwellers (*incolas*) inhabitants or parishioners to present a proper person to act as curate who had hitherto been accepted and admitted by the Dean and Chapter. That forty odd years before the Dean and Chapter duly commended one William Smallwood to the said Curacy which Smallwood the parishioners and inhabitants did mislike of and they or the greater part of them did elect and nominate another Minister George Eveley (Yeaveley) Clerk[2] to serve the said cure and did notify the Dean and Chapter and thereupon the said Smallwood was displaced and the said Eveley admitted by the Dean and Chapter to the place of Curate of the said Church.

That the said Edward Cresswell was nominated and elected by the residents, inhabitants and parishioners or

---

1. It was evidently desired to emphasise the parochial character of the Church.
2. The Yeaveleys in the 16th and 17th centuries were landowners in the parish, and had property at Whitehough Head and also on the north side of the Market Place, including the Old Hall, now the Roebuck Inn.

the major or senior part of them, but the said Thomas Barney had hindered him in performing the duties of the said cure from October to January last, all of which was well known and could be proved and he (Cresswell) prayed for relief.

The Capitular authorities appear to have ignored this appeal for the next document is a copy of a Petition addressed to Sir Francis Bacon, Lord High Chancellor of England, by George Thornhill and Robert Gibbe,[1] Churchwardens, on behalf of themselves and of other parishioners and inhabitants within the said Parish. The petition is lengthy, but is important as setting forth succinctly the method of election and nomination which the petitioners alleged had prevailed time out of mind. The evidence of old inhabitants that we shall presently quote takes the custom back to the edge of the Reformation period, and goes to disprove views that have been expressed that the right of the inhabitants did not arise until after the suppression of the Priory of Lenton which Priory, it has been suggested—on the ground that it held the greater part of the tithes—possessed the Advowson. There seems indeed to be no foundation for such a suggestion and the petition distinctly states that the Dean and Chapter held the *Rectory* which was appropriate to them. No doubt the intrusion of the Countess of Shrewsbury in 1577 was an attempt on the part of that indefatigable lady to claim a share in the advowson as part of the property of the Priory acquired by her former husband, Sir William Cavendish, but the fact that she concurred with the Chapter in nominating a Minister and that, her claim being denied by the

---

1. George Thornhill, of Warmbrook : a descendant in the senior line of the Thornhills of Thornhill, in the parish of Hope. This branch settled at Warmbrook in the 15th century, and was one of the leading families in the parish until 1733, when Warmbrook and other properties were sold. Dr. Clegg makes many references to the family in his diary, and deplores the dissipation and extravagance of the George Thornhill of his day. Robert Gibbe, of Bagshaw Hall, represented another old family. Hugh Gibbe was witness to a grant of land at Bagshaw in 1423.

Parishioners, she does not again appear on the scene, shows that her case was a very bad one—if she had any case at all.

With some slight modernisation of spelling the Petition runs as follows:—

> "Humbly complaining show unto your honourable good Lordship your Orators George Thornhill and Robert Gibbe Churchwardens of the Parish Church of the Chapel of the ffrithe in the High Peak in the County of Derby for and in behalf of themselves and of other the parishioners and inhabitants within the said Parish, That whereas there is and time whereof the memorie of man is not to the contrarie hath been an ancient parish Church or Chapel within the Parish of Chapel in the ffrithe the Rectorie or parsonage of which said parish is and time whereof the memorie of man is not to the contrarie hath been appropriate to the Dean and Chapter of the Cathedral Church of Lichfield in which church or chapel time out of mind of man there hath been and used to be and so of right ought to be a chaplain minister or curate maintained to celebrate Divine Service and Sacraments and all other rights of holie church for the Parishioners and inhabitants within the said Parish which chaplain minister or curate time whereof the memorie of man is not to the contrarie hath used to be chosen and placed there in the manner following that is to say, That when the said Church or Chapel hath been at any time void then the Churchwardens of the said Church for the time being and all the parishioners and inhabitants within the said parish or so many of them as have been so thought fit have used (upon public and usual warning given in the said Parish Church or Chapel beforehand) to meete and then and there by the common consent and agreement of the said Churchwardens and of all the said inhabitants then present or

the greater part of them to elect and chose one to be their chaplain minister or curate there, which chaplain minister or curate so elected and chosen the said Churchwardens parishioners and inhabitants or the greater part of them have time whereof the memorie of man is not to the contrarie used to nominate unto the Dean and Chapter of the Cathedral Church of Lichfield to be by them the said Dean and Chapter allowed and placed as Chaplain minister or Curate in the said Church or Chapel into the same and in the manner and form the Chaplains ministers or curates have been nominated allowed and placed in the same Church or Chapel time out of mind of man which said ancient custom and use of chosing nominating and placing of the said chaplaine minister or curate there ' hath bredd much quiet contente and comforte to all the said p'eshoners and inhabitants within the said pishe. But nowe soe it is maie it please yr Honorable good Lpp' that William Tooker Doctor of Divinitie Deane of the said Cathedrall Church of Litchfield Daniel Purye clarke one of the Prebends or Cannons of the said Church of Litchfield John ffulnetby clarke and other of the Prebends or Cannons of the Church of Litchfield and the Dean and Chapter of the said Cathedrall Church, having conceaved some causeles displeasure againste yr orats and the rest of the said pishions or againste divers of them or els out of a covetous desire to inriche themselves doe now of late refuse to allow or to place anie one in the said pishe church or chappell which yr orators and the said pishons shall nominate unto them the said Deane and Chappiter publishing and affirming that they maie place in the same what pson or chapplaine shall please themselves."

The petition then goes on to say that the said church or chapel had recently become void by the relinquishing

THE RIGHT OF PRESENTATION 67

or departing therefrom of Francis Barney, late chaplain, minister or curate, and the Petitioners and the rest of the Parishioners according to their ancient custom, meeting all at or in the Church upon usual and public warning had elected and chosen " one Edward Cresswell a learned religious and reverende preacher " to be their chaplain and, according to their aforesaid ancient custom, nominated him to the said William Tooker, Daniel Purye and John ffulnetby and the said Dean and Chapter and " did in curteouse and friendly manner request them to allow and place him in the said Church which " they (the Dean and Chapter)

> " did expressly refuse to doe affirming that they might place there whom they would at their pleasure and that they would place there an other one of their choice nominated and allowed to be chaplain minister or curate in the said parish Church or Chapel which they had since done accordingly,"

viz., one Thomas Barney, Clerk, who was then placed in the said Church accordingly.

"And whereas the said Deane and Chapter of Litchfield time whereof the memorie of man is not to the contrarie have used to repair and so of right ought to repair the Chancel of the said Church or Chapel which is now in greate decaie and if the same shall not be speedily repaired will verie shortly fall downe and be quite ruinated the same standing in a country where there be verie few churches and much tempestious and ill weather and if the said Channcell should fall downe the fall thereof would indanger to bring downe the whole churche the said William Tooker, Daniell Purye and John flulnetby and the said Dean and Chapter have utterly refused and still doe refuse to repaire the same although they have been thereto oft-times requested by your orators and for as much as your orators not being incorporate have no remedie by the comon lawes of this lande to compell " the said Dean, etc., " to allow and place the said Edward Cresswell who was chosen and nominated by your orators and the reste of the said pishoners and inhabitants according to their aforesaid auncient custome and usage nor to remove the said Thomas Barney . . . ."

Here the manuscript stops abruptly at the end of the eighth page, the remainder having been probably destroyed by damp and age.

On the 25th March, 1618, Raphe Ashenhurst, Esquire, and Edward Pegge, gentleman, with two other Commissioners sat at Chapel-en-le-Frith to hear evidence in this suit. That taken on behalf of the Plaintiffs has been preserved, from which it appears that they called twelve witnesses. There are two copies of the Interrogatories ordered to be administered to the witnesses the nature of which will be gathered from the evidence set out below.

The interrogatories vary slightly in detail—one set probably being suggested by the Plaintiffs and the other the official queries ordered to be put by the Court. Some of them were not answered in the copy of the evidence before us, so will be noticed here.

The witnesses are to be asked, amongst other things : whether the Dean and Chapter of Lichfield had paid " £8 yearly stipend or wages to the minister or curate of Chapple parish?" and what other yearly allowance do they give him?

Whether the Dean, Dr. Tooker, refused to allow Mr. Cresswell as Minister " saying that the nomination and election of the said curate belonged to the said Dean in right of his Church and that his predecessors had had it and he would not loose it from his possession or used some words to that effect."

Whether the Dean did " find any fault or take any exception to the insufficiency of the said Edward Cresswell or object against him that he was too *yonge* or no

THE RIGHT OF PRESENTATION

minister?" And whether his only objection was that the Dean and Chapter and not the parishioners had the right of election.

"Whether is the said Edward Cresswell a minister and a man of honest and sober conversation? and one that applyeth his studdy and preacheth diligently and behoveth himself to the likeinge and good example of his neighbours?"

Whether the Dean and Chapter have exercised episcopal jurisdiction in the parish and whether the parsonage is impropriate to them.

Whether a document produced dated 3rd November, 1617, is the nomination of the Churchwardens and Parishioners of Edward Cresswell to the living.

The witnesses are enjoined to "Declare the truth according to your knowledge."

The questions as to the stipend and as to the jurisdiction of the Dean and Chapter are struck out and are not answered.

Twelve witnesses were examined on oath and much of the evidence is of course repeated by each. They were:

GEORGE YEAVELEY. Formerly Curate of Chapel and then Vicar of Glossop, whose name has already been mentioned. Aged 71. Had known the Church for 50 years. Caused the letter of 3rd Nov., 1617, to be sent. Recollects at least seven Ministers.

NICHOLAS WILSON: of Chinley, Husbandman, aged 86, has known the Church "all the time of his remembrance." Recollects that some 40 years before when Sir[1] George Mellor was minister "one Slacke came and

---

1. The term "Sir" or "Dominus" is, in some parish registers, applied to vicars or chantry priests, and usually implies a non-graduate. At Grasmere the tithe-taking rector is termed "Master," and bears the suffix "Clerk," while "Sir" is reserved for the curate, his deputy, who has not graduated at either University. This view is upheld in Dr. Cox's *Parish Registers of England*, p 251. It will be observed in the following depositions that the prefix is applied to some of the ministers named and not to others, the inference being that those not so styled were graduates.

acquainted the Parishioners that he was placed minister there by the Countess of Shrewsbury and Dean of Lichfield, and that thereupon the parishioners or the most of them went into the Chancel of the said Church and there conferred together concerning the same and thereupon the said parishioners then told the said Slacke that neither the said Countess nor the Dean of Lichfield could nominate or place a Minister or Curate to serve the said cure at Chapel-en-le-Frith without the consent comendation or nomination of the said parishioners or the greatest part thereof for the time being and that by custom and usage there the same parishioners or the greatest part thereof for the time being ought to elect nominate or comend a fit man to serve the same cure when and so often as the same was void or to that effect and that thereupon the said Slacke departed and the said Sir George Mellor continued curate or minister as before."

CHRISTOPHER MORE of Horwich, yeoman, aged 78.

NICHOLAS BROWNE the elder, late of Matlock, but then of Little Ridge, alias Banke, Esquire, aged 70,[1] THOMAS MELLOR of Town End, Yeoman, aged 33, JOHN WHITE of Tunstead Milton, Husbandman, aged 76, THOMAS MOULT of Eccles, Gentleman, aged 60,[2] THOMAS BAGSHAWE of the Ridge, Gentleman, aged 48, and THOMAS BAGSHAW of Chapel, Clerk of the Church, aged 34, all depose to the general custom and that they and others have been "moved" by clergymen who desired to become minister on vacancies occurring.

GEORGE BOWDEN of Bowden, gentleman, aged 70, goes into more detail as to the mode of procedure showing that the chief landowners had great weight in the

---

1. The Brownes, of Marsh Hall, who also owned Little Ridge (Bank Hall), were an ancient and influential family settled at Marsh since the 14th century.

2. It is interesting to note that of all the persons mentioned in these depositions Mr. Moult alone is now represented by direct descendants owning the same estate.

selection of a candidate. He says that when the benefice became void Mr. Browne, Mr. Bagshawe and himself or their ancestors have considered of a fit man for the said cure and that they and the rest of the said inhabitants or the greatest best or chiefest gentlemen and freeholders of the said inhabitants or parish have nominated chosen or comended some fit man to be minister and have presented him to the Dean and Chapter who have allowed or inducted such person. He remembers the Slacke episode, but his account is not so picturesque as Nicholas Wilson's. He simply says Slacke " came and would have been Minister " but because he had not or could not get the goodwill of the parishioners he was rejected. All the witnesses agree that Francis Barney was duly nominated by the parishioners, but that Thomas—although his brother, canvassed Mr. Bagshawe and some others—was placed as Minister by the Dean and Chapter without the consent of the parishioners and contrary to the ancient usage.

Two technical witnesses, JOHN TRAVIS of Moslie Hall, " ffreemason," aged 60, and JOHN HURDFIELD of Chinley, Carpenter, aged 33, give evidence as to the state of the Chancel which they say is in great ruin and decay both in the glass windows roofs battlements stone walls and timber work and unless it is soon repaired it will fall down so as to endanger part of the Church, and they add that the Church stands in a windy and tempestuous place or country. Several of the witnesses corroborate this and Messrs. Bagshawe, Browne, Bowden and Moult state it is now very fearful and terrible to be in or for people to pass in or through the same. They believe that the Dean and Chapter ought to repair the Chancel and when Sir George Mellor did some repairs the Dean allowed the cost " which was paid by some of the Dean's farmers[1] or to that effect."

Mr. Moult adds that when he was Churchwarden he

---

1. *i.e.*, the lessees of the tithes.

petitioned the then Commissioners to move the Dean and Chapter to repair the Chancel. Mr. Browne has also heard that the Minister for the time being ought to allow the Dean or his Farmer 40 shillings yearly towards the repair.

All these witnesses declare that they are not parties to the suit nor have they subscribed to the costs of either party. Nicholas Wilson, the oldest witness, recollects ten Ministers, Sir Thomas Armitage (c. 1538), Sir William Hyde, Sir Edward Bagshaw, Christopher Beard, William Smallwood, George Yeaveley, Sir George Mellor, Henry Brownell, Francis Barney, and Thomas Barney. Some of the witnesses mention Sir Henry Wylde after Beard, others omit Wylde and add Hyde, and with the exception of Sir Thomas Armitage the names as stated by Wilson are repeated by the other witnesses according to their ages, but not always in the same order. The title " Sir " is applied very loosely to practically all the ministers by one or other of the witnesses and does not appear to be of much value.

The evidence taken before this Commission satisfied the Dean and Chapter as to the rights of the Parishioners, but there is no record that at this or any other time have they taken any part in the repair of the Chancel.

The Church safe contains a document dated 25th April, 1620, under the Chapter Seal in which Dr. Tooker declares that for ever thereafter it shall be lawful for the major or senior part of the parishioners freely to nominate and elect an able and sufficient curate to read prayers and execute Divine Service and administer the Sacraments there and upon their election and nomination the Dean and Chapter to admit and license the same Curate.

The problem as to who were " the major and senior part of the parishioners " has, however, exercised the minds of succeeding generations right down to the present time.

THE RIGHT OF PRESENTATION

On one subsequent occasion, in 1747, the question of the right of nomination again became acute. At some period after 1617—there is no record as to how or when, but probably immediately after the receipt of the last-mentioned Declaration—a species of standing Committee of 27 Freeholders, nine from each " Edge," was constituted—a wise precaution evidently intended to prevent any repetition of the former troubles. In course of time this Committee practically took upon themselves the functions of the whole body of parishioners until their duties very nearly became a recognised right.

In 1697 the Rev. Caleb Cook was nominated by this Committee on the resignation of the Rev. William White, who had been for many years " disordered in his mind." Mr. Cook died on 6th August, 1717, and the Dean of Lichfield, Dr. Kimberley, considered the election of his successor of sufficient importance as to require his personal attendance at the meeting which took place—not in the Church or Vestry but at the Royal Oak Inn. There were three candidates and the Rev. John Byron, who had " served the cure very much in Mr. Cook's illness" was chosen by a large majority and the Dean declared him duly elected. The next Minister, the Rev. Benjamin Bardsley, secured the office by a bit of rather sharp practice. We are told that when Mr. Byron lay a-dying in February, 1727-8, Mr. Bardsley sent a man to bring him word when he did die and immediately on that notice Mr. Bardsley set out to Lichfield and got the place.

The parishioners were greatly offended at this, and if " some paper " had not been mislaid or lost they would have kept him out of the Church, some of the parishioners saying they would rather have spent £100 than that he should have the place in such a manner. Mr. Bardsley went so speedily and privately and got licensed that the freeholders had no time to consider what they would do, but it was quite expected that there would be a law-suit.

Mr. Bardsley, however, would have made an excellent modern politician for "*notwithstanding his license* he treated and made all the interest and friends he possibly could in the parish after he came in order to keep the parishioners quiet, and promised very fine things and how good he would be and what great things he would do in the parish for its benefit, and so it put the freeholders out of all thoughts of a suit." This is the story told by Edward Wood of Bagshaw, a slater, 84 years of age, in an affidavit made by him with reference to the appointment of Mr. Bardsley's successor in 1747, and he is supported in some of his statements by other old men, George Thornhill of Ringstones in Taxal, yeoman, aged 70, Joseph Swindells, a husbandman aged 80, and Robert Carrington, aged 75, both of Chapel. If we may trust the note in the Parish Register, Mr. Bardsley was a good Parish Priest, and kept his promises.

On Mr. Bardsley's death the Dean and Chapter again refused the Parishioners' nomination—the Rev. John Byron, B.A., then Curate of Over in Cheshire—and selected a young clergyman named Hand of Lichfield. The freeholders thereupon appointed a deputation who made two special journeys to Lichfield. (The Churchwardens' Accounts for 1748 show payments of £3 16s. 0d. to Mr. Samuel Kirk, and £8 8s. 10d. to Mr. Jasper Frith for money laid down and travelling expenses.) On the second visit the Chapter expressed themselves satisfied, but leave was given to Mr. Hand to disprove if he could the Parishioners' right, and the matter was referred to the arbitration of a Mr. Bonfoy of Ashbourne. Mr. Hand, however, found that he could not prove his case and withdrew his claim, Mr. Byron's nomination being accepted.[1] Thus ended the final attempt on the part of

---

1. *A propos* of this nomination, Mr. William Bagshawe, of Ford writing to his nephew, Colonel Samuel Bagshawe, M.P., expresses his opinion that the general practice of the inhabitants is to exercise their patronage in favour of "the worst man they can find to the best of their knowledge!" *The Bagshawes of Ford*, p. 184.

THE RIGHT OF PRESENTATION 75

the Capitular Authorities to over-ride the Parishioners' rights.

An inscription on a board formerly affixed to the west wall of the Church, but now relegated to the chamber beneath the belfry, sets out some of these facts and further that Mr. Byron was licensed at the nomination of the major part of 27 of the chosen inhabitants or parishioners, and those who made the nomination agreed on the death of any one of their number to choose a successor.

It will have been observed that nothing is said in the proceedings in the case of *Thornhill* v. *Tooker* about the 27, and the earliest reference to them that we have met with is in the Parish Register for 1624-5, Feb. 20, " Edmund Nickson was chosen minister of this Church with the consent of the most part of the XXVII Freeholders of our parish."

During the ninety years following Mr. Byron's appointment this Standing Committee was kept up and at length the members seem to have *bonâ fide* considered themselves the patrons until 1836 when, on the death of the Rev. Samuel Grundy, there was a contest for the vacant benefice.

The Parish Register contains records of several meetings held during the latter half of the eighteenth century for the election of Freeholders to fill up vacancies in " The Twenty-seven." In 1790, after public notice, "the persons who claimed the right of presentation to this living disallowed Robert Bennett as admitted amongst the number, his property being copyhold." In 1792 Peter Bramwell is admitted on the death of George Goodman, Esq.

Doubts having been cast on the authority of the Twenty-seven to nominate, the opinion of Dr. Stephen Lushington was taken in 1836, who advised that the Committee had been originally appointed not for the purpose of nomination solely but to perform all the material business of the parish, and that the right to nominate a curate was vested in all the parishioners above 21, assessed to Church and Poor Rates. This view was substantially confirmed by the opinion of Mr. Arthur (afterwards Lord Justice) Charles in 1885, and again in 1891 by that of Sir Walter (now Lord) Phillimore. The latter advised that the electors were rated occupiers of full age including those occupiers who paid rates through their landlords, *i.e.*, the same franchise as for a Parliamentary, or now for a County Council, election. These opinions were acted upon in the elections of 1836 and 1901. It remains to be seen whether the Parochial Church Councils Measure 1921, sec. 4 (1) (i) will affect the question. The Diocesan Authorities appear to consider that it will as the Southwell Diocesan Kalendar states the patrons to be " the Parishioners by the Parochial Church Council."

On the death of the Rev. S. Grundy in 1836 there were three candidates for the vacant benefice. On the day of election, St. Thomas Day, 1836, the parishioners assembled in the vestry of the Church at 9 a.m. Some resolutions as to fees to be taken by the Minister and "abolishing for ever the Popish custom of claiming mortuary or corpse presents" and other more or less irregular resolutions were passed. The candidates were then formally proposed: the Rev. George Hall, B.A., by Thomas Goodman,, Esq., and Mr. Edwin Oldham; the Rev. Bernard Moore of Derby by Thomas Gisborne, Esq., M.P., and Mr. Peter Booth, and the Rev. Edward Hewlett of Sheffield by Messrs. John Marchington and Isaac Hallam. The poll was opened immediately and continued till 4 p.m. when the result was declared to the parishioners in the Chancel by Mr. John Lomas, the Chairman of the Vestry Meeting, as follows: Hall, 278; Moore, 99; Hewlett, 4. An old parishioner, the late Mr. Philip Marchington, graphically told us how when a boy he came with his grandfather George Potts of

THE RIGHT OF PRESENTATION

Plumpton, then 95 years of age who, declining to be driven to the poll, walked down from Plumpton and back again. The poll was taken in the ordinary manner of the day, each voter going into the vestry and declaring for whom he voted. Carriages were freely used and partisans of each candidate closely scrutinised the poll, but so far as Mr. Marchington recollected there was no treating. After voting most of those present adjourned to the Bull's Head Inn where there was much eating and drinking and some fighting!

No other contested election took place till 1901 when it was conducted in a seemly manner at the usual polling places in the parish and in strict compliance with the law observed at Parliamentary and other elections.

On the two last vacancies an Advisory Committee of twenty-seven has been appointed at a meeting of the rated occupiers and six candidates selected by this Committee have been invited to preach "trial sermons" before the actual nominations were made.

CHAPTER VI.

THE CHAPLAINS OR MINISTERS.

IT is much to be regretted that it is not possible to formulate any authentic list of the chaplains or incumbents. Dr. Cox accounted for this in his day on the ground that Chapel being one of the Peak parishes within the peculiar jurisdiction of the Dean and Chapter of Lichfield, no Episcopal confirmation was required to make the appointment to the benefice valid. Consequently the Lichfield Episcopal Registers afford no information. Such registers must have existed in the capitular records, but recent enquiry has not been successful in discovering them.

We are therefore obliged to content ourselves with such gleanings as can be gathered from various sources, and it must be borne in mind that—with the exception of Thomas Armitage (1434), Nicholas Dikson (1457-77), and Stephen Bagsha (1521)—the fact of those chaplains mentioned in the following list prior to 1538 being parish priests of Chapel can only be a matter of conjecture. From 1538 to 1618 the names are to be found in the depositions in the case of *Thornhill* v. *Tooker*, and from 1620 onwards in the Parish Register.

The short tenure of so many of the ministers during the greater part of the sixteenth and seventeenth centuries is rather curious, and might lend colour to the suggestion that a new régime prevailed—for a time at least—after the Reformation whereby the parishioners made the appointment for a short period and provided the greater part of the stipend as in the Dartmouth instance,[1]

---

1. See p. 48.

THE CHAPLAINS OR MINISTERS 79

and the notes in the Parish Register on the appointments of William Oliver and William Higginbottom might be quoted as bearing this out were it not that the former's ministry continued for two or three years and only terminated with his death. A probably better solution lies in the miserable stipend which alone would be a good reason for seeking a better preferment at the earliest opportunity. Several times between 1624 and 1662 occurs the entry " noe minister."

1339. WILLIAM BUCSONE, Capellanus, mentioned as a tithe payer in the Capitular Receipt Roll for this year (Derby Arch. Soc. Journ., xi, p. 142).

1350. THOMAS DEL CLOUGH, nominated by the Queen (Philippa) into the Chaplaincy of Chapel-en-le-Frith " annexed to the Church of Hope." A Commission was issued by the Lichfield Chapter to their official Dom. Peter Scarleston, Canon of Lichfield, to aid in repelling this intruder, iiii Kal., July (28 June), 1350 (Jeayes, p. 80). Thomas probably retained the living for in 36 Edward III (1362) Thomas del Clough " Clico " witnesses a grant of land in Hordron and le pursecloghes (? Peaslows) in Bowden.[1]

1408. JOHN ALOT, described as " Chaplain " in grant by John Bradshaw of lands in Bowden 6 May, 9 Hen. IV (1408) (Jeayes, p. 81, Bowles MSS.).

1430. WILLIAM BROME and GEOFFREY BAGSHAWE, described as " Chaplains " in grants by them of lands in Bradshaw and Lightbirch dated Feast of S. Mark, 8 Henry VI (25 April, 1430). (Jeayes, p. 81, Bowles MSS.)

1434. THOMAS ARMITAGE, " Chaplain of Chapel en ly Frith," took a lease from the Dean and Chapter of

---

1. From the Hassop Charters, communicated by Mr. E. G. Bagshawe.

Lichfield of the tithes and Altar dues of Chapel and Fernilee. Rent £8. Dated Dec. 1434. (Jeayes, p, 81.)

1450. SIR RANDULPH BARLAWE,[1] described as "Chaplain" in grant by William Boler of lands in Bagshaw dated 30th Nov. 29 Henry VI (1450). (Jeayes, p. 81, Foljambe MSS.)

1457—1477. NICHOLAS DIKSON. Mentioned several times between these dates. Described as "parish chaplain of Chapel-en-leFrith" in grant by Nicholas Bowden dated 8th April, 17 Edward IV (1477). In 1483 was Parson of Claxby, Lincolnshire. (Jeayes, pp. 81, 82, Bowles MSS., Wolley MSS., and P.R.O.)

1521. SIR STEPHEN BAGSHA, "curatt of ye Chapell in ye Fryth" witness to the will of Henry Bradshaw of Bradshaw Hall, dated 2nd March, 1521. (Jeayes, p. 83, Bowles MSS.)[2]

1523. EDWARD DEAN, chaplain, with Nicholas Browne de ly Marsche held a lease from the Dean and Chapter of the Fee farm of Chapel dated 18 July, 1523. (Jeayes, p. 83.)

1538. THOMAS ARMITAGE, "capellanus capella in ly Frythe," had a lease from the Dean and Chapter of the tithes of Chapel and Fernilee dated 26th July, 1538. (Jeayes, p. 83.) Called "Sir" Thomas in depositions.

(?) WILLIAM HYDE.

155-. EDWARD BAGSHAWE, witness to marriage settlement of Richard Kirke of Whitehough and Helena Kirke de la Courseys, 11 Nov., 1 and 2 Philip and Mary (1553).[3]

---

1. See note 1., p. 69.
2. Another witness was Sir John Bredbery, "owre Lady prest."
3. He may have been the second son of Thomas Bagshawe of Ridge by Florence, daughter and heiress of Thomas Cockayne of Ashbourne. See *The Bagshawes of Ford*.

THE CHAPLAINS OR MINISTERS

CHRISTOPHER BEARD.

1571. GEORGE YEAVELEY,[1] resigned and became Vicar of Glossop.

1574. GEORGE MELLOR,[2] on resignation of George Yeaveley, called " Sir " in the Depositions which state he became Vicar of Ilkeston.

1577. HENRY BROWNELL.

FRANCIS BARNEY. Resigned in favour of his brother, Thomas Barney.[3]

1616. THOMAS BARNEY. Ousted by Edward Cresswell.

1618. EDWARD CRESSWELL, B.A.

1620. WILLIAM BRAY, made first entry in Parish Register 3rd Dec., 1620.

1623. RICHARD EATON.

1624. EDMUND NICKSON, Feb. 20th "was chosen minister of this church with the consent of the most part of the XXVII Freeholders of our Parish." P.R.

1645-6, Feb. ROBERT GEE, M.A., resigned Nov. 1648, and became Vicar of St. Peter's, Derby, but returned Dec., 1651.

1648-9. WILLIAM OLIVER. " March 24 began this year March 18th."—P.R. The Parliamentary Commission appointed in 1650 report " Mr. William Oliver present incumbent and disaffected." Buried in the Chancel 6th Dec., 1651.

1651. ROBERT GEE. Buried in the Chancel 1 May, 1652.

---

1. The Dean and Chapter selected William Smallwood to succeed Christopher Beard, but the parishioners upheld their right to the appointment of their nominee, George Yeaveley, a local man. See p. 63.
2. Again the Dean and Chapter, this time in conjunction with the Countess of Shrewsbury, nominated "one Slacke," but withdrew him on the objection of the inhabitants.
3. In 1656, Francis Barney, Minister of Woodfield (Worfield), Shropshire, was present at the marriage of Richard Shallcross, of Shallcross Hall, at Hope.

1652. THOMAS CLEATON (*alias* Clayton).
1660, Feb. JAMES HULME.
1663. WILLIAM HIGGINBOTTOM. "Feb. Hired to serve the cure of Chappell for one year." (P.R.)
1668. JOHN MORWOOD.
1669. NATHAN KINSEY.
1670. WILLIAM WHITE, M.A. Carved the oak Altar Rails now in the Baptistery. Became "disordered in his mind" and retired in 1697 on a pension of 4/- per week from the Churhwardens.
1695. FRANCIS NABBS or KNABBS.[1]
1697. CALEB COOK. "Mr. Caleb Cook who was Curate of this church 20 years and some more departed this life the 6th day and was buried in the Chancel above the steps on the south side of the table the ninth day." (P.R., 9 August, 1717.)
1717. JOHN BYRON. Buried in the Chancel 12 February, 1727. His wife Mary and a still-born child were respectively buried in the Chancel on 17 and 13 November previous.
1728. BENJAMIN BARDSLEY, B.A., Oxon., on death of John Byron.

1747-8, Jan. 12th. "This day The Rev. Benjamin Bardsley, A.B., of Brazen Nose Coll. in Oxford was buried under the Communion Table in the Chancel. Twenty years he watched over his flock with yt Integrity and vigilance which became a Labourer in the Vineyard of X^t insomuch that whin

---

1. It does not appear that he was actually the minister, but he seems to have acted during Mr. White's indisposition. The Apostle of the Peak, who was expecting to meet him at a funeral, wrote in his diary on 2 March, 1695/6, "I desired to be serious in all companies and 'especially' in the company of Mr. Nabbs who takes much liberty in his discourse and is jovial in his carriage. I write this with a sense of my own frailty." *The Bagshawes of Ford*, p. 23.

ye space of a fortnight before his death when he was administering ye Holy Sacrament to his Parishioners tho' before he fainted twice under the Burden of his Duty y^t he shewed such marks of his great sense of y^t comfortable Feast y^t all were sensible y^t nothing less y^t an extraordinary Devotion of ye Supreme Deity could enable him to perform y^t duty. He lived an exemplary patern of Sobriety Honesty and Virtue preached in the Pathetick with Success and eminently distinguished himself by his learning in such useful parts of knowledge as are immediately necessary for ye ministerial Life—ye 9th he departed to the Grief of all such as admire the before-mentioned virtues." (Parish Register.)

1748. JOHN BYRON,[1] B.A. On death of Benjamin Bardsley, at that time Curate of Over, Cheshire.

"The Rev. Mr. John Byron who had been minister of this parish for upwards of 42 years, departed this life on the 5th November, 1790. When he first entered on this benefice the parishioners were engaged in litigious disputes which were terminated by his intercessions . . . . . he always studied the interest of his Congregation by going hand in hand with them on all publick occasions and might in the words of the Poet be justly esteemed ' one of the noblest works of God '—an honest man. (Parish Register.)

1790. WILLIAM BAGSHAWE, M.A. Resigned in 1792 and became Vicar of Wormhill.

1792. SAMUEL GRUNDY. On resignation of Wm. Bagshawe.

---

1. Dr. Clegg notes on 11 June, 1748, "Young Mr. Byrom (sic) has at length got the Curacy of Chapel and there has been ringing and great rejoicing for it." He was probably a son of the former minister, but we have found no mention of this.

1836. GEORGE HALL, B.A. On death of Samuel Grundy.
1885. SAMUEL HENRY PINK. On death of George Hall.
1891. JAMES GIVEN, M.A., LL.D. (T.C.D.). On death of Samuel Henry Pink. Resigned January, 1901, and became Vicar of St. Saviour's, Nottingham.
1901. JOSIAH CLIFTON STREDDER, M.A., Oxon., on resignation of James Given.

CHAPTER VII.

THE CHURCH OFFICIALS.

THE CHURCHWARDENS.

THE following list is taken from the Register from 1622 onwards. From the residences it may be gathered that the wardens were like other parish officers selected from the three "edges" in something like rotation. A few instances occur of non-residents being appointed which would be in respect of occupation of property in the parish.

There is nothing to suggest any deviation from the usual, and present, mode of nomination of one Warden by the Minister and the other by the Parishioners, but the person nominated was obliged to act although he could appoint a substitute.

c.		
1610	Thomas Moult of Eccles[1]	Thomas Kirke
1617	George Thornhill	Robert Gibbe
1622	Humphry Lowe	Thomas Mellor
3	Thomas Allen	Nicholas Lomas, Smith
4	Ralph Gee	Edmund Mellor
5	Henry Bagshawe	Robert Taylor
6	George Bagshawe of Combs Head	Henry Dayne of Alstone Lee
7	Nicholas Bagshawe of Wilkinhill	Thomas Dakin "de milne"
8	Thomas Mellor of Townend	Edward Taylor of Eaves
9	Arnold Kyrke of Martinside	Thomas Lomas of Dane Hey

---

1. A lineal ancestor of one of the present churchwardens, Col. Goodman, C.B., D.L.

1630 Thomas Walklate   Nicholas Kyrke of Lane
  1 Thomas Greensmith   Nicholas Yonge
     of Brook
  2 Thomas Cooper   Henry Lomas of Flatt
  3 John Bennett of Light-   William Carrington of
     birch   Eccles
  4 Thomas Greensmith   Thurston Kyrke of Bow-
     of Maglow   den Head
  5 Nicholas Cooper   Richard Lowe
  6 John Bagshaw   Anthony Crosley
  7 John Shirte   Thomas Barbor, Junr.
  8 John Lowe   Ottewell Lowe
  9 Nicholas Lowe   William Marchenton
1640 Charles Ashton   Thomas Kyrke of Mille
  1 Charles Ashton   Thomas Kyrke
  2 Raphe Bagshawe   Anthony Bealott
  3 Ralph Bagshawe and Anthony Bealott, Church-
Dec.   wardens, but did no service.

3/4 Mar. This year we have no Churchwardens.

4/5 Feb. Noe Churchwardens.[1]

1647 George Bowden   Anthony Cresswell
        "They served not."
  8 George Bowden of   Anthony Cresswell of
     Lanesyde for Bow-   Blackbrook
     den Edge
1650 George Bowden   Nicholas Cresswell
  1 Humphrey Marshall   Thomas Allen
  2 Edward Ollerenshawe   William Carrington of
            Bings
  3 George Thornhill Junr   Thomas Lowe
  4 Nicholas Bradshaw   John Heathcote
     Junr
  5 Thomas Moult of   John Bennett of Whit-
     Eccles   hough
  6 Robert Gibbe Junr   George Kirke

---

1. A similar entry appears in the register at intervals till Feb. 1649-50, after which there is no reference to wardens till Sep. 1653. The names, where given in the intervening years, are taken from the List of Parish Officers. Probably during the Civil War and the Commonwealth the wardens were duly elected by the vestry, but were not admitted at the Visitation.

THE CHURCHWARDENS

    7 Robert Crosley   Thomas Astireman, Thornilee
    8 Edward Wright of Horwich   Nicholas Smith of Chapel
    9 George Bagshaw of Hollenknowle   Thomas Tayler, Eaves
1660
    1 Henry Kirke of Courses   John Cowper of Higher Courses
    2 John Carrington of Blackbrook   Thomas Lomas, Eaves
    3 Henry Daine, Jur. of Alstonlee   Edward Lomas, Thornilee
    4 William Yeaveley   John Crosley
    5 Humphrey Thornell   Edward Cresswell
    6 Henry Bagshaw   George Mortin
    7 William Moult of Further Milton   George Marshall of Newfield
    8 William Lingard   Thomas Waterhouse for Bowdenhead
    9 George Lowe of Alstonlee   Edward Wright of Baghouses
1670 Francis Gee for Roeside   Thomas Gee Jun : for Lydgate
    1 Thomas Greensmith of Maglow   George Sherte of Bowdenhead
    2 Nicholas Lomas Jun : of Thornilee   Robert Marshall for Bank Hall
    3 Edward Kryke of Whitehough   Nicholas Lingard of Stodhart
    4 William Tunstead for Lomas Land   Edward Dixon for Cresswell Land
    5 George Marshall for Hurst   5 John Ollerenshaw of Tunstead
    6[1] John Bennett   Francis Taylor of Laneside
    7 Thomas Mellor   George Kyrke of Waterside

---

1. In each of the years 1676, 77 and 78, the name of Robert Browne is substituted in the Register for the first name in the List of Officers, in 1679 the Register gives Henry Kyrke and Robert Browne. In 1681-83 the Register gives John Downes in place of the first name.

CHAPEL-EN-LE-FRITH PARISH CHURCH

    8 Thomas Moult for Bridgefield
      George Mortin for Bridgefield
    9 John Kyrke of Laneside
      Francis Taylor
1680 John Downes of Laneside
      Nicholas Cresswell of Blackbrook
    1 Henry Kirke of Martinside
      Thomas Cowper of Owlgreave
    2 George Cowper of Wilkinhill
      Thomas Moult of Whitehough
    3 Arnold Kirke of Mill
      Henry Trickett
    4 Ralph Bagshawe of Hordron
      Reginald Turner of Baghouses
    5 John Bagshaw of Further Bradshaw
      Nicholas Lowe of Cockyard
    6 Thomas Barber of Malcalf
      John Greensmith for Rushop and Richard his brother for Brook copartner
    7 John Downes
      Robert Bradley
    8 Francis Mosleye of Lightbirch
      John Bennett of Silkhill
    9 Ralph Marchenton of Eaves
      Thomas Frith of Slack Hall
1690 Henry Longden of Daneheyhead
      George Morten of Bridgefield
    1 William Cowper
      John Lingard
    2 John Kirke of Malcalf
      Edward Sherte of Clough
    3 Anthony Bealott
      John Bramwell for Combs Edge
    4 Robert Moult Under Eccles for Geo: Thornhills land
      John Downes, hired for Ollerenshaw
5 & 6 Mr. John Hall of Hope
      Wm. Lees of Townend
    7 Thomas Marshall
      George Allen
    8 Robert Bagshaw of Marsh Green
      Henry Kirke of Chapel
    9 George Thornhill
      John Shert
1700 Ralph Dain
      John Mortin
1 & 2 Mr. German Buxton
      George Thornhill
    3 Robert Wainwright
      Joshua Wood
    4 James Lowe
      Ralph Mortin

THE CHURCHWARDENS

5 & 6	John Carrington	Edmund Warrington
7	Robert Wainwright	Anthony Ward
8	William Jackson	John Brocklehurst
9	Edward Garnett	John Lomas
1710	Robert Bagshaw	John Walker
11	William Cooper	Stephen Bellott
12	Mr. John Shallcross	Mr. Thomas Bagshawe
13	James Carrington	Robert Thornhill
14	Lewis Bagshaw	Ebenezer Middleton
15	William Higginbotham	Ebenezer Middleton
16	Elias Hall	William Storer
17	Henry Bagshaw	Ralph Hudson
18	James Ford	George Cooper
19	John Godwin	William Jackson
1720	Henry Lomas	James Lowe
1	William Hudson	William Janney
2	John Fletcher	Joshuah Shirt
3	John Hall	John Fletcher
4	Matthew Walker	John Fletcher
5	John Wainwright	John Marchington
6	John Fletcher	John Marchington
7 & 8	John Hall	Edward Holgate
1729 & 30	John Fletcher	Henry Lomas
1	John Shirt	John Wainwright
2 & 3	Jasper Frith	John Wainwright
4	John Lingard	Joseph Millard
5 & 6	John Frith	Henry Ward
7	Daniel Woolley	Robert Ollerenshaw
8 & 9	John Fox	Matthew Lee
1740	Robert Creswell	George Bowden
1 & 2	Henry Lomas of Flatt	Richard Turner of Baghouses
3	John Watkinson	Hugh Garside
4 & 5	Henry Kirk	John Marchington
6	Samuel Wilde	John Fox for Wm. Bradbury
7	George Brocklehurst, Ollerenshaw	John Fox for John Lowe, Horwich
8	Thomas Bowden	Adam Jackson
9	Robert Holdgate, hired Ewd. Holdgate	Abraham Yates

1750	Nicholas Kirk	Cornelius Pickford
1	Edward Holdgate	John Shirt
2	Henry Bagshaw	John Kirk
3	James Pickford	John Dronfield
4	John Shirt, Junr	Benjamin Longden
5	Stephen Bellott	John Pickford
6	Edward Bennett	Thomas Ford
7 & 8	,, ,,	Samuel Wood
9	Edward Walton	Thomas Middleton
1760	John Lomas	Robert Hudson
1	Edward Dain	Peter Turner
2	Edward Bennett	Matthew Lee
3 & 4	,, ,,	Thomas Marchington
5	,, ,,	Robert Bagshaw
6	,, ,,	Thomas Pott
7	Abraham Yates	Francis Vernon
8	Edward Bennett	William Ashby
9	,, ,,	Robert Bagshaw
1770	,, ,,	John Pott
1	,, ,,	Joseph Heginbotham
2	,, ,,	James Carrington
3	,, ,,	Isaac Lomas
4, 5, 6	,, ,, (Senr Surgeon)	William Pott
7, 8	William Pott	John Fox
9	John Shallcross	Joseph Bennett
1780	William Carrington	Josiah Fox
1	William Yates	John Lomas
2	George Heathcote	Robert Yates
3	William Lingard	Thomas Orgill
4	Robert Hibberson	John Shallcross
5	William Lingard	Cornelius Pickford
6, 7	William Potts	Edward Green
8	Septimus Olerenshaw (Pyegrave)	Wm. Sutton (Haslehurst)
9	John Fox	Edward Green
1790	Wilfred Curwen	James Storer
1	Cornelius Pickford	John Frith
2	,, ,,	William Ward
3	William Ward	Robert Bennett
4	Stephen Bellott	Henry Bagshaw
5	John Goddard	Thomas Lomas
6	Robert Bagshaw	,, ,,

THE CHURCHWARDENS

7	Josiah Bradbury	James Lomas
8	Anthony Shallcross	Jacob Lomas
9	James Goddard	Henry Lomas
1800	,, ,,	John Lomas
1, 2	Thomas Bagshaw	John Booth
3	Henry Morten	Philip Olerenshaw
4	William Shepley	Thomas Hide, Jun[r]
5	Robert Kirk	Philemon Rowbottom
6	Adam Fox (Spire Hollin)	Isaac Lomas
1808	John Howe for John Slack	Peter Kirk
1809	John Howe for John Dixon	Peter Kirk for John Thomasson
1810	James Walton	Ralph Turner
1811	John Howe for Thos. Hartle Junr.	Thomas Lomas
1812	William Yates	William Bailey
1813	Job Righton	John Heginbotham
1814	Robert Hibberson	Thomas Marchington
1815	William Thomasson	Adam Mortin
1816	Thomas Reddish	James Lomas
1817	Jasper Needham	John Bagshaw
1818	Stephen Bellott	Adam Fox
1819	George Chappell	John Howe for Samuel Ford
1820	Robert Hampson	George Chappell for Henry Kirk
1821	George Chappell for Henry Mortin	John Howe for John Beard
1822	Thomas Goodman, Esq.	George Shepley
1823	John Howe for Peter Merrill	Robert Bagshaw
1824	John Howe for John Dixon	George Chappell for John Vernon
1825	James Gaskell	John Watts
1826	James Shallcross	John Howe for John Bramwell
1827	Stephen Joule	George Heathcott
1828	Thomas Wyld	Thomas Bargh
1829	Thomas Wyld	George Hadfield for Joseph Hadfield

1830	Mr John Frith	John Bennett
1831	Edwin Oldham	Joseph Carrington
1832	Anthony Bellott	John Williamson
1833	Josiah Bradbury	Adam Fox
1834	Thomas Goodman Esq	John Ibbotson
1835	John Marchington	John Hall
1836	John Frith Esq	John Lomas
1937/9	Edwin Oldham	Robert Marshall
1840	James Ward	John Bramwell
1841	Edwin Oldham	Samuel Lowe
1842/3	John Bagshaw	Samuel Needham
1844	Mr Vernon	Adam Fox, Spire Hollins
1845-7	Davenport Goodman	John Potter
1848-52	,, ,,	Henry Kirk
1853-56	,, ,,	Anthony Bellot Jackson
1857	,, ,,	Thomas Clayton Bennett
1858-9	Robert Hill Hyde	Henry Kirk
1860-5	Thomas Kirk	John Grime Hughes
1866-9	Anthony Bellot Jackson	John Boyd
1870-4	William Hy. Greaves Bagshawe, J.P.	John Boyd
1875-80	William Hy. Greaves Bagshawe, J.P.	Anthony Bellot Jackson
1881-3	Davenport Goodman	,, ,, ,,
1884-5	Joseph Heathcott	,, ,, ,,
1886-96	,, ,,	James Cooper Hyde
1896-8	John Burton Boycott	,, ,, ,,
1898—1902	Samuel Needham	,, ,, ,,
1903	Samuel Needham	John Taylor, J.P.
1904-8	James Cooper Hyde	,, ,, ,,
1908-9	William Stirling Anderson	,, ,, ,,
1910	John Bennett	,, ,, ,,
1911-13	Robert Righton	Francis Bramwell
1914-17	Alexander Young	,, ,,
1918		,, ,,
1919	George Herbert Pink	,, ,,
1920-5	Col. Godfrey Davenport Goodman, C.B., D.L.	,, ,,

The Churchwardens' Accounts.

In the vestry is preserved an old book containing numerous accounts and entries concerning the Church and also Civil matters pertaining to the Parish generally, a relic of the time when the Churchwardens had many powers and duties covering a wide range of parochial affairs. Interesting as this book is we are now only concerned with it as it deals with purely Church matters. Some of the earliest items, going back to 1661, are receipts for the Earl of Devonshire's share of the Corn and Hay Tithe—£8 13s. 4d.per annum. These are sometimes given as paid by the Minister and sometimes by him for the Inhabitants and are signed by the Earl's Agent or Collector and countersigned by the Parish Clerk or the Churchwardens. This payment was made annually at the Wakes, and in the eighteenth century the Wardens usually enter in their accounts " spent with the Corn tithe men 2/6 " which, in 1731, they say was " according to custom."

This book contains the Churchwardens' annual accounts from 1700 to 1725, but unfortunately they only give totals and no details.

The Account of Ralph Hudson and Henry Bagshaw for 1717 may be taken as typical:—

Received

			£	s.	d.			£	s.	d.
Seat lay	1 being insolvent	...	13	0	0	Disbursed		19	06	6½
Land lay	1 ,, ,,		9	6	2½	In their hands to pay		04	05	6
Of Old Churchwardens ..			1	05	10	Succeeding Churchwardens				0½
		tott	23	12	0½		tott	23	12	0½

Apparently a seat lay and/or a land lay was levied as required, the latter being the precursor of the more modern Church Rate.

A bundle of Accounts from 1729 to 1786 is in existence, and from about 1800 onwards the accounts have been regularly kept.

We have had occasion to refer to some of the payments—the accounts are in many ways interesting, but are much too long to allow of more than a selection of typical items being made. It will be noticed that throughout the eighteenth century little business was transacted without something being "spent."

1729
March	19	Paid to John Plat for taking down ye Steeple	10	10	6
May	22	A fees and charges at Visitation		18	2
	29	King Charles ye 2nd Restoration		9	0
		Spent when ye old Churchwardens made their accounts		9	7
June	11	King George ye 2nd Inaugn. spent		11	8
	15	King George ye 2nd Proclamation		6	0
		Spent at Rushbearing	1	8	4
		Spent when ye Schollars were nominated		2	6
Aug.	24	Spent on Mr. Barbon and Mr. Birks wⁿ yʸ came to preach		6	2
Oct.	8	Spent at Signing Briefs		1	6
	11	Spent Coronation of King George ye 2nd		11	2
	18	Pd. Mr. Kirk[1] for Micmas Sacrament wine		8	0
		Spent ye same day		2	8
Oct.	30	King George ye 2nd Birthday		6	0
		pd. Jos Swindells ye same day for trees and setting em		4	2
Nov.	5	pd Ringers and spent		12	1
		Spent when Mr. Sheldon and ye freeholders made agreement with Mr. Bagshaw		10	5

---

1. Landlord of the Town Head (King's Arms) Inn. At this time wine, as at Chesterfield, cost two shillings per bottle.

THE WARDENS' ACCOUNTS

	13	Spent with the apparitor		8	3
		pd ye same day for ½ a pint of wine			6
	27	Pd for Geo Bramal's coat		10	0
		Court fees at ye 2nd visitation		18	7
Dec.	9	Spent when poor cloth was divided		5	0
		Spent with ye freeholders on St. Thomas's Day		4	0
		Spent on Xtmas Day		5	0
	28	Pd James Pickford[1] his ½ year's wages	3	0	0
		Pd to Mr. Kirk for Wine for Xmas Day and Sunday follow		12	0
Jan.	19	Spent on Prince of Wales Birthday		5	0
		Given a poor man		1	0
Mch.	20	Spent when we had an assessment made		1	8
		Pd Francis Frith for gathering stone			6
		Pd to Mr. Clows[2] for Sacrament wine for Good Friday and Easter Sunday		14	0
		Spent on Easter Sunday[3]		2	6

1. The parish clerk.
2. Landlord of the Royal Oak Inn.
3. These items are of considerable interest. It would appear from the accounts that Holy Communion was celebrated on Easter Sunday, Whit Sunday or Trinity Sunday, at Michaelmas, Christmas Day and the Sunday following, and also on Good Friday. The wardens charge expenses on these days, which in later accounts vary from 8d. to 5s., no sum then being fixed as was the case in some parishes. In 1732, 6s. was charged "for six Sacrament dinners to the Churchwardens as usual," and in 1802 15s. as "expenses on six Sacrament days." In 1818 the "annual allowance" is £1 10s. The Good Friday celebrations are somewhat unique. Dr. Cox, who had no knowledge of these accounts, says Chesterfield is one of the few instances that he found where Good Friday celebrations can be proved right through the eighteenth century. (*Derbys. Arch. Journ.*, xii., p. 165). At Chapel, however, they continue to the present day. The wardens expenses were paid for a long period, *e.g.*, "March 27, 1806, expenses on Good Friday being a Sacrament day 5/-" and six Sacrament days are mentioned in 1818.

	Pd. last Visitation for Books for alteration of prayers		4	0
	Spent ye same day at Bakewell		2	10
	Pd mending ye clock		5	0
	Spent on Easter Tuesday		3	0
	pd. for Hedgehogs and Ravens		13	10
	pd. for a post letter from Wolverhamton			10
	pd for two ladders for ye use of ye Church	1	0	0
	pd James Pickford his ½ years wages and his bill	4	13	5
	pd for writing two presentments		1	0
	pd for writing accounts		2	6
	pd more to Mr. Fitzherbert his charge	2	2	0

1731
May 11   Ct. fees and charges and expenses of Minister and Wardens at Visitation obtaining a Brief for the repairs of the Church   1 3 8

     12   Spent on ye Ringers when ye Brief came to hand   5 0

     30   Princess Caroline's Birthday   5 0

Given to a poor man with a letter of request   1 0

July 9   Spent with corn tythe men according to custom   2 6

(The Wardens made several journeys to inspect Towers, etc., during this month.)

Spent on ye road to Oldham 2/-
In drink same night 2/6   4 6

Breakfast next morning 1/6 our horses 3/- and gave to ye maid and ostler 6d. each
That morning in wine 1/-   6 6

		Our dinners at Ashton 2/6 for ale and beer at dinner 1/6	4	0
		Our horses and ye Ostler	12	0
		Spent from Ashton to Chapel and on ourselves and Horses at Chapel	3	6
		For horses ye journey	no charge	
Aug.	11	pd. Thos. Frith repairing ye Church gate 2 days	2	0
		Spent on a many freeholders at Robt. Ridgeways who came there to view ye candlestick and to see whether it was according to bargain and for fetching ye same	12	0
	14	Paid in exchange of our Candlestick	15 0	0
Oct.	22	Princess Ann her birthday	5	0
		pd Ezekiel Shuttleworth for ye Communion Table	1 1	0
		Princess Looisa's Birthday	5	0
Mch.	1	Queen's Birthday	5	0
		pd Henry Kenion 5/- for two load of lime and couching 1/6	6	6
		Pd for ye use of a large pair of scales to weigh ye Bells with and carriage from and too Stockport	2	6
		Spent when we consulted with the freeholders whether Mr. Bagshawe should see ye instrument about seat lays	4	0
		pd for gravelling schoolyard	3	0
		pd two poor men with a pass or letter of request	1	6

A Foxhead		1	0	
Badgers Heads		6	0	
Hedgehogs 2d each and Ravens 4d each	1	4	3	

1732
July 26 Pd ye same day (at Visitation) for a Pennance letter for Eliz. Ford[1] — 8 0

Pd. Mr. Clows' Bill of Charges when ye Revd ye Deane of Lichfield was here &c. — 7 17 9

Spent at Rushbearing according to Agreement — 15 0

Spent at Townhead when ye Articles for Southside oth' Church were executed — 3 0

Pd for making a new Surplice — 10 0

Spent upon ye Glazier — 6

Given Winifred Bagshawe — 6

Nov. 5 Pd. ringers — 10 0

Coal for Bonefire — 1 0

Pd. Mr. Ludlam in exchange betwixt ye old weather-cock and ye new one — 2 12 0

Spent at same time — 2 0

Pd. Geo. Brammall 2 days wages for cleansing ye Church — 1 4

Pd. for a New Common Prayer Book — 16 2

Gave 8 men who had been took prisoners by ye Turks — 1 0

---

1. Penance in Church was common in the eighteenth century, but this is the only case we have met with at Chapel. The penitent usually appeared bareheaded and barelegged, clad in a white sheet. There is no reference to this case in the P.R.

Pd. for a double post letter from
   Mr. Rudhall   1   0
A wisket for ye use of ye Church $2\frac{1}{2}$
Pd. for 12 load of Buxton Lime   11   0
Pd. Mr. Hand for attending ye Court to justifie ye election of ye present Churchwardens notwithstanding Jos. Trickets caveat   2   2   0
pd. George Thornhill (according to agreement at a vestry meeting) for ye loss of his horse   3   9   0
pd. ye Workmen for taking up ye seats on ye South side of ye Church and laying up same carefully on ye Beams in ye Belfry   3   0
Spent on Geo : Ward and others who assisted in weighing ye old lead wch. belonged to ye South side of ye Church   2   8
Spent when Winifred Bagshawe's goods were valued   1   0
Ravens Heads 5/- Badgers 2/- and Foxheads and Hedgehogs   7   0 / 11   4
pd. Geo : Platt towards Southside oth' Church   50   0   0

1734   pd Hezekiah Bennitt, Joseph Ashton Jno Ashton Thomas Frith each a day's wages for working in ye Churchyard   3   0
pd. Elizabeth Bowden for mending surplice   8

Aug. 22   Spent when ye last payment for ye Bells was discharged   1   6

Nov.	pd. Geo. Brammall his wages for walking i'th Church[1]	10	0
	pd. Ezekiel (Shuttleworth) for mending the Bier		10
	pd. Ezekiel for mending the rails at the Communion Table	2	8
1737	Spent when Mr. Pott of Taxal was here with ye Freeholders[2]	3	6
	Pd. Jno. Warrington for mending ye Black	1	0
	Pd. Mr. Mundy a Sollicitor and Agent for the late officers and for ye parishioners of this parish the contents of a Bill mentioned and allowed in ye sd. accounts amounting to the sum of[3]	19 14	6
1740 Nov. 28	Pd. and spent when the officers and Inspectors met about the Poor House	3	0
	Spent in consulting about putting out an apprentice[4]	1	0
1742-3	Spent when we bargained with Mr. Platt about Church Gates	1	6

---

1. He would be the sexton. In many churches the sexton or other officer was employed to keep order and turn out dogs. He was sometimes armed with a long wand to awake sleepers.
2. Edward Pott, B.A., Rector of Taxal, 1723-53.
3. See p. 155.
4. The churchwardens had various Poor Law duties now devolving on the Guardians of the poor. They were parties to all apprenticeship indentures. *e.g.*, 1st July, 1730, the churchwardens, John Fletcher and Henry Lomas, and the overseers of the poor placed Elizabeth Wilson, "a poor child of the said parish," as apprentice with Isaac Clayton, of Silkhill, until she should be twenty-one or marry, to be taught "the art and skill of Housewifery." The children were often of tender age: for instance, in 1799, Peggy Ford, aged eight, is sent to Rowarth to learn "the art of spinning and manufacturing cotton wool."

THE WARDENS' ACCOUNTS

	Spent on Disley Ringers		2 6
	Washing new Surplice twice		2 0
	pd for putting up the Stone Pitt[1]		1 0
	pd. for dressing Candlestick		9
	pd. for whitewashing the Church	1	5 0
	Gave the stone getters at 2 several times in drink		2 0
	pd. pulling down the Church style and redding groundwork for the peers		3 6
	pd for hewing and setting up ye Peers	10	8 0
	pd John Hall for ringers drink on a Holy Day		5 0
	Pd. Mr. Walker for a tab and lace		1 6
1744	Pd. about Balguy Lad		2 0
	Pd. Edward Ward for Mossing Katty Cooper house		1 6
	Pd. John Armstrong for 6 foot of wood and for two days work		9 8
	Gave him in drink		2
	Pd. the ringers when the good news came that we had gotten the Battle at Deginton (Dettingen)		5 0
1745	Spent when Motheram Ringers were here		2 6
	Pd. Sarah Holdgate about green garland[2]		1 0
1747	Spent with Mr. Bardsley and Mr. Slack when we bargained with him to varnish ye Pictors in Church	0	3 0

1. This may have been the stone circle near the church gates.

2. As is well known, a custom prevailed in many Derbyshire churches of hanging up a garland in memory of young people. This is the only reference we have found in Chapel.

	Pd. Mrs. Bocking for the new serplis	1	3	1½
	Pd. Mrs. Bardsley[1] for making the serplis		10	0
	Pd. for exchanging the new Salver	2	4	4
	Pd. Mr. Slack his bill for varnishing Pictors in the Church of Mosses and Eron[2]	1	10	0
1748	Pd. Mr. Worthington's Bill[3]	23	3	5
	Gave to a poor man yt played Tunes upon ye bells		1	0
	Cowpapers and forms of prayer[4]		10	0
1749				
25 June	Spent upon Curate of Edale		1	4
10 Sept.	Spent upon those who assisted us to disperse ye Nutters from nutting on Sunday		1	6
1750	Spent on Good Friday with Parson and Freeholders		3	4
	Pd. to ye Masons for 4 Rood of walling at the Bone house at 3/6 per rood		14	0
	Pd. for 4 rood of stone at 7/6	1	10	0
	Nails and cords for ye Altar frames			2

---

1. The minister's wife.
2. These have now disappeared. Sir Walter Besant, in an account of the Church of All Hallows the Great, Thames Street, London, describes similar pictures as forming part of the Reredos, Moses on the right pointing to the Ten Commandments, and Aaron on the left in full Pontificals.
3. Apparently in connection with the right of presentation.
4. A severe cattle plague or "pestilence amongst the horned cattle" raged in England from 1745 to 1755. Cox, *Derbyshire Annals*, ii, p. 292, sets out a prayer ordered in 1748 to be used in churches throughout England "every day on occasion of mortality among the cattle." Dr. Clegg makes several references to the outbreak, and mentions cases at Rushop Edge.

Aug.	pd. to John Mellor for 35 days work in liming washing and pointing Church and Chancel	1	15	0
	Allowed John Mellor half a pint of ale per day		2	11
	Pd. for necking ye surplice		1	10
1751	Pd. Eben. Pickford's Bill for casing the beam under Moses and Aaron		12	6
	pd. George Bagshaw for Altar Frames	1	4	0
	Hy Kenion for Painting and guilding ye altar frames and for painting ye case under Moses and Aaron	1	10	0
	Henry Ward's Bill New lead 10 c. 2 q. 13 lb. at 16/6 is	8	15	2
	Old lead 76 c. 1 q. 6 lb. at 2/6	9	10	11
1751	Pd for 5 load of lime		2	11
	pd. for slecking of same			10
	The new black and making of it was	1	14	0
	Repg. ye old black		1	8
1752	John Pickford's Bill for sacrament wine on Good Friday	1	4	0
	To ye Ringers for bluffing bells		2	6
1753	Gave the Chimney Sweeper lad to go away			6
1754	Pd. to Robert Holdgate for keeping boys out of the Churchyard		5	0
	Pd. for Bread and Beesoms		1	6
	pd. for a basin for ye font			3
	Spent pulling down ye partition between church and chyard		1	3
1755	Spent when the Minister of Taxal came to preach here		4	0

	Spent when Mr. John Frith's money for burying in Linnen was distributed to the poor	2	8
	Pd. George Bramwell for wipinge and walking in Church on Sunday	10	0
	Pd. for a Bible and Common Prayer Book	3 6	0
	Pd. for carriage of 'em and laces affixing to them	2	10
1756	Form of Prayer for ye Fast Day	17	8
	7 Lime trees planted in the Churchyard	7	0
	Four more at	3	0
	Pd for carriage of the Trees and setting them	0	11
	pd. Robt. Holdgate for Sacrament bread and Beesoms	1	6
	Packthread to repair ye Matts before ye Altar		2
1757	pd. for blew paint for the candlestick and canopy rods	5	6
	Mr. Ewd. Byrom's bill for Table Cloath and Furniture	1 0	5
	Pd. for two bundles of Moor silk for Matts.	2	6
	George Wright's Bill for leather for Pulpit cushion	5	0
	Do for 5 pounds of feathers for it	6	3
	Pd. for a form of prayer for taking of Louisbourgh	1	6
1758	Given to Morris Dancers at Rushbearing	3	0
	Robert Bagshaw had for Rushes		6
1761	Gave a boy for fetching the Churchwardens (apparently when the Apparitor came)		6

1762	Gave Mr. Swaine a Treat when he preached here	2	10
	Pd for 13 Lime Trees for Churchyard	16	3
	Pd for carriage of them from Manchester	1	0
	Gave to the Carrier in drink 2d. getting them 1/- in drink, etc.	1	4
	pd for three forms of prayer on several occasions	5	0
1763	Pd for the Thanksgiving prayer for the Queen's safe Delivery and Birth of a son	2	0
1764-8	The accounts for these years include many items relating to the erection of the hearse house.		
1766	Pd. for an Umbrella	10	0
	Pd. for a napkin for the Altar	2	10
	Spent with Parishioners in valuing ye Hearse	4	0
	Pd. the Bill for the Hearse harness and two setts of Bobs and other things thereto belonging	12 8	3
	Spent in going twice to Castleton and twice to Sheffield	5	6
	Other items show that in addition to the above, £9 8s. 3d. was spent upon the Hearse. As there are no earlier entries it would appear that the Parish Hearse was first provided at this time. The Hearse House still stands in Market Street. Receipts for hire of the hearse outside the		

Parish occur in subsequent accounts, *e.g.*, "2/6 for hearse into the Forest" and "5/- for the Hearse for fetching Mary Gee from Bank End to Ashton Clough and thence to Chinley Chapel."

1772					
Nov.	5	Given the boys for the Bonfire			6½
1778		pd. John Frith's Bill for ceiling and plastering Church and Chancel as agreed	30	0	0
1780		John Ford's Bill for the new black for Bier	5	5	3
		Pd. Mr. Pickford for a dale plank		5	0
		Pd. Organist	2	5	0
1781		Wm. Shepley for painting figure board		5	6
		pd. for Surplice 12¾ yds at 2/6 per yard Irish Cloth	1	19	6
1783					
Aug.	24	Pd for a cartload of Rushes for Church		6	0
		Pd for half a hundred of bricks			9
		Pd for a license and bond for a 3 penny Tax upon Baptisms Marriages and Burials		6	6
		Pd. for John Harrop's Top coat and making	1	5	9½
		Jno Harrop's years wages	1	1	0
		John Braddock for a sprittle handle			5
1785		pd. for the furniture of the vestry and carriage 4d.		12	4
1801		Wm Smith for two foxes	1	2	0
		Singers at Charity Sermon		2	6
		Adam Slack for Jas. Ford's Hat		19	0

THE WARDENS' ACCOUNTS

Year	Item	£	s	d
	James Ford Clothes	3	10	0
	Messrs. Simms for repairing and tuning organ	10	10	0
1803	Beautifying and repairing the Altar Piece	3	19	4
	Expenses of a Rush Cart	2	2	0
	Ale for Workmen since January	1	7	9
1805	Salary to P. Bramwell for blowing bellows	1	0	0
1806	Expenses on putting up the Commandments		2	0
	pd. Wm Shepley his bill for writing and gilding the Commandments	5	0	0
1818	Amos Potts, Wm. Smith and Jos Barton for killing 7 foxes	2	11	6
	Robt. Cottrill and Jos Lowe, Hollin for 3 Hedgehogs		1	0
	Robt. Holdgate, Clerk, for his Journey to Tideswell to bring back part of the surplice which had been stolen, including his expenses		4	9½
	Annual allowance to the Churchwardens for their attendance at Church on 6 Sacrament Days	1	10	0

THE PARISH CLERKS.

Prior to 25 March, 1617 (then æt. 34). THOMAS BAGSHAW. Buried 26 June, 1646.

July, 1646. HENRY BAGSHAW, nominated by the Rev. Robt. Gee. Buried in Chancel 13 Feb., 1655-6.

3 March, 1655-6. THOMAS BAGSHAW. Note in Parish Register That Thomas Bagshaw of Chapel being

chosen Clerk of the parish by all or the major part of the Freeholders and inhabitants of the said parish before divers faithful people of the Commonwealth at Bakewell was sworn Register of the said parish. Buried in Chancel 22 March, 1680-1.

THOMAS BAGSHAW is mentioned in Parish Register as Parish Clerk in November, 1681, and May, 1682, but there is no other reference to him. His is probably the burial in the Chancel on 23 August, 1683.

P.R., April, 1684. "Notand That through want of a Clerk some occurrences in this month were omitted, but they are here beneath inserted."

3rd March, 1684-5. ROBERT MOULT. Sworn before the Surrogate at Bakewell. Buried in Chancel 24 Jan., 1687-8.

October, 1687. WILLIAM BRADSHAW.

169-. JAMES PICKFORD. Buried 12 Sept., 1729.[1]

17 July, 1735. JAMES PICKFORD. Nominated by Rev. B. Bardsley.

1st March, 1760. ROBERT HOLDGATE.

1790. CORNELIUS PICKFORD.

1792. GEORGE BRAMWELL, nominated by Rev. W. Bagshawe.

1806. ROBERT HOLDGATE, nominated by Rev. S. Grundy.

1828. ROBERT HOLDGATE.

GEORGE BRAMWELL.

July, 1841. PETER BRAMWELL, who died 5 Jan., 1895. In addition to his clerkship Mr. Bramwell was, during a long life, identified with many religious and social activities in the Parish. Since the death of Peter Bramwell no Parish Clerk has been appointed.

---

1. Dr. Clegg attended the funeral. "He was a quiet, diligent, honest man and, I hope, a good Christian. His death is a wide breach."

The Sextons.

The family of Bramwell can claim an even more lengthy association with the Church as Sextons than their friends in the Belfry, for since 1631 the post has been practically hereditary. On the Sexton's workshop in Dane's Yard adjoining the Churchyard may be read, carved in stone, the following inscription :—

"Charles Bramwell, Died 1878, and was Sexton of Chapel-en-le-Frith for 24 years, His father 43, His Grandfather 50, his great-grandfather 38, his Great-great-grandfather 40, his great-great-great-grandfather 52."

The Parish Register records the burial on 6 February, 1720-1, of "George Bramwell, Sexton of this church who had been sexton near 40 years."

Charles Bramwell, mentioned above, was succeeded in 1878 by his nephew Joseph Bramwell, who with a short interval (when his brother James Bramwell acted) was Sexton until his death in 1910, when he was succeeded by his nephew Tom Bramwell. On the latter, who was a member of "B" Coy. 6th Batt. Sherwood Foresters (T.F.), being mobilised on 4th August, 1914, his father Peter Bramwell took up the duty temporarily, but Tom being killed in action at Kemmel in May, 1915, Peter Bramwell became Sexton and so continued till his death in January, 1923, when he was succeeded by a younger son, James Bramwell, the present sexton.

CHAPTER VIII.

THE PARISH REGISTERS.

THE earliest existing Register commences 3rd Dec., 1620, and there is no trace or sign of any previous one—indeed with the exception of Hope (1599) and Bakewell (1614) it is the oldest in the High Peak.

The inscription at the beginning of the first Register suggests that there was none earlier; it runs:—

> "Registrum seu liber Registrarum occurrentum omnium in parochiali Ecclesia Capella in le Frith ab anno incarnationis 1620. Guil: Bray tunc temporis ibidem curato."

The first volume covers the period 3rd December, 1620, to 15th November, 1698. It contains about 2,730 Baptisms, 2,980 Burials, and 295 Marriages. The excess of Burials over Baptisms is probably accounted for by the fact that many non-parishioners were buried and that some baptisms—at any rate in the latter part of the period under review—would take place in nonconformist places of worship.

In addition to the Register proper the book contains interesting lists of the "officers of the Parish both for the Church and King," *i.e.*, the Churchwardens, Overseers of the Poor and Surveyors of Highways, and also particulars of money collected in the parish on Briefs.

Mr. Thomas Bowden of Bowden Hall commandeered two pages, one in 1652 and another in 1662, and inserted particulars of marriages of members of his family, not only recording the issue of these marriages but giving the names of Godparents and other details, and from other evidence there is little doubt that the entries were

THE PARISH REGISTERS

made personally by him. Some of the entries are in Latin in a cramped hand, probably that of the Rev. Robert Gee, minister, 1645-48.

The second volume commences 10th Nov., 1696, and ends 14th May, 1745. The third volume, which is in a very dilapidated state, many pages being loose, carries us to 1792. After Mr. Byron became Minister in 1748 the register is better kept and generally well written, but is much more business-like and omits the little personal notes of the earlier books. The fourth Register takes us to 1806 after which the entries are on printed forms in formal style.

Amongst names frequently occurring in the first Register are :—

Allcock, Allen, Ashenhurst, Ashton, Bagshawe, Bennett, Beard, Barber, Barker, Bayley, Bore (Bower), Bowden, Bradbury, Bradley, Bradshaw, Bramwell (Bramall, Bramhall), Browne, Braye, Buxton, Biver, Brearley, Bowler, Barrott, Bealott, Birchenough, Botham (Bottoms), Carrington, Cooke, Cresswell, Clayton (Cleaton), Cowper (Cooper), Crookes (Crux), Crossley, Cotterill, Cheetham (Chitom), Cartlache, Clarke, Chapman, Collier, Downes, Dayne, Darnell, Doulphin, Ellis, Frith, Fletcher, Fullalove, Foxlowe, Gee, Gibb, Greaves, Greene (Grine), Greensmith, Goodwin, Hall, Hallam (Hallom), Hadfield, Hill, Hinchcliffe, Heathcote, Heaward, Hawkesworth, Hesketh, Howe, Hyde, Holland, Jowle (Gowle), Jodrell, Jackson, Kenordyne, Keye, Kirke (Kirk, Kyrke), Kinder, Lees, Leonard, Lingard, Lomas, Lowe (Low), Marchenton, Marshall, Mellor, Moore, Morton (Morten, Mortin), Mosley, Moulte, Needham, Newall, Newton, Ollerenshaw, Olliver, Palmer, Pedley, Peake, Penyngton, Platts, Ramscarr (Ramisker), Richardson, Rowbottom, Rowlinson, Royland, Shallcross, Shatwell, Shirt (Shert), Shipley, Shore, Slacke, Smith, Stafford, Straightbarrel, Stirlinge, Swann, Swindells, Taylor, Thornhill, Townsend, Tunstead,

Turner, Vernon, Waterhouse, Ward, Walklate, Warhurst, Warrington, Watts, Whildon, Whitle, Whyte, Wigstone, Wilson, Willshaw, Winterbottom, Wood, Wyott, Yealott (Elliott), Yeveley, Young.

This list is by no means exhaustive. Many came from Peak Forest and a few from Fernilee, Taxal and other places. Until the Church of King Charles the Martyr was erected at Peak Forest most of the Baptisms, Marriages and Burials from that Township must have taken place at Chapel and throughout the Registers many entries relate to inhabitants of Chinley, Bugsworth and Brownside; in fact, as we have noticed in Chapter IX., the rather unusual custom prevailed of numerous families from this Township having burial places within the Church.

After 1754 the Marriage Registers are kept separate and are in the conventional form required by various Acts of Parliament.[1]

A perusal of the early registers suggests that few children were unbaptised—even those of vagrants and wayfarers received the benefit of the rite. We may hope that in these cases this was more by reason of the universal recognition of the duty of parents to their children than of the vigilance of the parish officers. An early entry is:—

" 15 July 1651, George son of Richard and Mary Barker being poor people that lay at the Chapel Milne,"

and there are many similar entries relating to the children of " poore travellers " or " a poore wandering woman." One on 2 July, 1685, reads:—

" A child found near the town end whose parents were unknown was baptised and called John."

---

1. The Marriage Registers down to 1837, abstracted and edited by the present writer, have been published by Phillimore & Co. Ltd., London, 1914, in *Phillimore's Parish Register Series, Derbyshire*, vol 12.

THE PARISH REGISTERS

A sadly large percentage of baptisms are those of illegitimate children, the name of the " reputed father " being almost invariably given. A pathetic feature is the number of still-born children, recorded amongst the burials, too often accompanied both as to these and as to others who survived by the entry of the mother's burial—both lives no doubt sacrificed to a lack of medical and sanitary knowledge. The context suggests that as a rule baptisms took place within a few days of the birth. At times quite a number of children or older persons—not infrequently husband and wife—from the same hamlet are buried within a few days of each other, evidently pointing to the presence of epidemic diseases, which, as Dr. Clegg's Diary shows, were very prevalent in his day, some, such as smallpox and " a bad fever," being practically endemic.

An occasional baptism or marriage outside the parish is recorded, and amongst others there are two references to baptisms having taken place at " the neawe Chappelle of Shallcross." On 7th Dec., 1623, is entered " Thomas son of Robt Lomas of Ryeflatt," and on 27th February, 1623-4, " George son of John Wright of Baghouses." It is, however, worthy of note that on 15th Dec., 1624, Elizabeth, daughter of John Shallcross, was baptised at Chapel Church.[1]

Several baptisms by the Rev. William Bagshawe, the Apostle of the Peak, are also noted. John, son of George Bagshaw of Hollin Knowle, was baptised in Church on 18th March, 1689-90, and on the 30th of the same month is a similar entry, " baptised by Mr. Bag-

---

1. These entries are rather puzzling. The "new chapel" could hardly have been a dissenting place of worship at that date. The Rev. W. H. Shallcross does not mention any chapel at Shallcross Hall, but Cox (*Churches*, iv, p. 508) says there was a chapel attached to the Hall which subsequently came to be regarded as a semi-parochial one for that district, and seems to have been never used after the time of the Commonwealth. If it was in existence in 1624 it is curious that Mr. Shallcross should have his daughter baptized at Chapel Church, but she may have been born at the Old Hall in the Market Place.

shawe " 31st Jan., 1696-7. Nathaniel, son of Saml. Bagshawe of the Ford, " was baptised by his grandfather."

Some items give more intimate details as :—

" 13 Aug. 1626. Randulphe son of Randulphe Ashenhurst Gent . . . . . but was born the last day of July being Monday about 5 o'clock in the morning."

" 8 Dec. 1645, Henry son of Peter Kirk the oldest of this town."

The parents' trades or occupations are sometimes given as " a tinkler "; " daughter of Edmund Rowe and his wife of Yorkshire being travellers and called by the name of pedlors." In the eighteenth century we find John Hardy, Peruke maker, and Francis Bottoms of Tunstead Milton, a " Sive maker," whilst Thomas Kirk, the father of Hannah Kirk, baptised 4 June, 1727, is " commonly called Nunckle Tom."

The baptism of Abraham, son of Anthony Bealot of Castlenaze, on Whit Sunday, 17th May, 1657, is correctly described as taking place on *White* Sunday. A few years earlier on 29 March, 1652, Dorothy, wife of Thomas Allen, was buried in Church " being Black Monday."[1]

There is nothing very striking in the Marriage Registers beyond the fact that throughout they are kept in rather slovenly fashion. An illuminating entry is " Robert Moulte of Whitehough married his wife the 13th daye " of July, 1636, no reference being made to the lady, and several omissions of Christian and surname of one or other of the parties occur. On two occasions the Rev. J. Byron carefully describes the bride as

---

1. Easter Monday. "It is to be noted that the 14 day of April and the morrow after Easter Day (1360) King Edward (III) with his host lay before the City of Paris which day full dark of mist and hail and so bitter cold that many men died on their Horsebacks with the cold; wherefore unto this day it hath been called Black Monday." *Stow's Chronicle.* Incidentally, it may be gathered from this record that severe weather in April is not a modern innovation.

"Widow and a Spinster." There is no explanation of the two following entries unless it be that one was a Civil Marriage. The Bagshawes of Hollin Knowle were Roman Catholics. "9 Jan. 1657-8, Thomas Bowdon of Laneside and Grace Bagshawe of the Hollin Knowle."

"14 Feb. Thomas Bowdon of Laneside married Grace Bagshawe of Hollin Knowle the 14 day and was married by Mr. Thomas Clayton minister of this parish."

"5 May, 1657, There came to Chappell from Tideswell and Litton 17 marriages all married by Randle Ashenhurst, Esq., Justice of the Peace."[2]

The Burial Registers at once draw attention to the great number of non-residents buried in the Churchyard and, more strangely, in the Church itself. Naturally many tragedies are recorded, and the danger of travel in the High Peak is brought home to us by the numerous deaths of travellers from accident or exposure.

7 Aug. 1622. Robert Lambe of Altrincham slain by a fall from his horse. He died in Fernilee. Buried in the Chancel.
6 Jan. 1623-4. A pore man found dead above the Ballgreave and was thought to have perished there.
5 April 1626. John Lomas of Thornilee who had lived in lunacie some 20 years.
30 Dec. 1626. Jonas France of Peak Forest slain in a grove (*i.e.*, lead mine. There are a number of such entries).

---

2. Of Beard Hall, the gentleman whose baptism we have noticed. Under an Act passed by the celebrated "Barebones Parliament" in 1653 marriages were to be performed by Justices of the Peace. In *The Civil Warres of Great Britain and Ireland* "by an Impartiall pen," published in 1664, we read "our Mock-Parliament who sat from July till December (1653) without having employed their authority in anything except the making of an Act concerning marriages and this out of meer envy to the Clergy." The impartial nature of this record is not obvious.

4 Feb. 1627-8. Anthony Barbor of Malcalf was drowned in the Priraccor Water[1] on Jan. 28, but was not found till 31st.

About this time are chronicled several burials at night —probably cases of fever or plague.

19 Feb. 1628-9. Henry Pedley a pore naturell foole.

A woman child was tabled (? boarded) at William Wyott's was buried 8 May, 1641.

5 Nov. 1647. Thomas Downs qui quedam mortuis de amputation cruris.[2]

6 July 1649. Charles son of Mr. George Bowden buried in ye Quire of ye North Ile.[3]

6 June 1653. Robert Newton, a young man living at Congerton, killed himself at Peaselache Cross (at the top of Sparrow Pit).

20 Sep. 1656. A poor child found dead in ye Forest.[4]

15 July 1661. An old man named Hugh died at Lead Knowle in Bugsworth, he was a stranger and usually sold tobacco as he travelled his surname is unknown.

Under date February, 1684, but evidently written later, appears the following rather sycophantic appreciation of Charles II :—

"Upon Friday the 6th of this month did our sovereign and most gracious Lord King Charles the 2nd of ever blessed memory depart this life having reigned six and thirtie years and a weeke to the getting

---

1. Probably at the ford at Smithbrook, where there was a close called Prior Acre on the north side. There appears to have been no bridge over Smithbrook until 1715. Several references are made in the register to "the Causeway," the houses opposite to the present Wesleyan Church, where the road was formerly sunk to come down to the ford.
2. *Crus* = the leg below the knee.
3. See p. 16.
4. This is the subject of a poem by Mr. Henry Kirke in *Derbyshire Ballads*.

himself great honour and love both in foreign parts and at home for he very much endeavoured the establishment of Peace justice and piety and by his wisdom was much prevalent therein. England did (as indeed there was great cause) very much bewail and lament the death and loss of so gracious a King. After his death the imperial Crown of England did lineally descend to his royal Highness James, Duke of York and Albany, brother to the late King who was crowned King of England etc. upon St. George's day being the 23rd day of April 1685."

13 April 1688. Barnabas son of Robert and Mary Bagshaw in Church.

21 April 1688. James son of John and Jane Fletcher. " noe affidavit was made for these two corpses."[1]

22 Nov. 1690. Thomas Clayton of Blackbrook was found dead in a stone pit of the Blackbrook Moor and was buried in the Churchyard having auctority for his interment from Mr. Ralph Adderley who was then coroner.

7 Oct. 1696. Mary Wife of Nicholas Shottwell of Bagshaw was buried at Slack Hall.[2]

20 July 1700. Elizabeth Wyott of Chapel Milton who was by the ancient of this parish supposed to be an hundred years of age.

5 April 1702. Mr. William Bagshaw of the Ford Nonconformist Minister in the Chancel. (A later hand has added "styled the Apostle of the Peak.")

26 April 1702. A poor traveller who went under the name of an Egyptian.

---

1. A statute of Charles II (1667) required all bodies to be buried in woollen shrouds for the encouragement of the woollen trade. By subsequent Acts of 1678 and 1680 an affidavit of compliance with the original statute was to be delivered to the priest under a penalty of £5. This penalty was, certainly in some cases in Chapel, given to the poor. See p. 104.

2. The Quakers' burial place within the park at Ford Hall.

15 June 1703. A young woman which came from Woodhead who had been at Buxton Bath as she was coming home suddenly fell off the horseback and in a little space dyed.

2 Jan. 1711-12. William Cooper of this town and Hannah daughter of Thomas Moult of Tunstead Milton who was both burned to death in their own house, he going as was thought to save the child's life lost his own life the last day of December and was buried he in the Church and she in the Churchyard.[1]

1 Feb. 1714-15. And that day their was an extream wind it blew the wether cock of the steple and broak it in peices and a great Ashe down in the Churchyard with vast great loss to most people in their houses some being blown down.

March 1716-17. An account of a mishap to a young girl named Phoenix who, setting out from Lane Side at Blackbrook to Peak Forest, was overcome by the snow on Peaslows and was buried in a drift for six days without any food, but seems to have been none the worse for her adventure.[2]

March 1717. This was a stormy spring for on the 30th is recorded what is evidently a fine display of Aurora borealis "it streamed up like unto long picks (? peaks) of great bignes."

---

1. The scene of this catastrophe seems to have been the site of the old "Hat and Feathers" Inn in Market Street. It was sold by Anne Cooper of Chapel, widow of William Cooper, plumber, in March, 1712. Dr. Clegg says the fire took place between the hours of 12 and 2 in the morning. He does not speak highly of Cooper's moral character, but notes that he had received the Sacrament that day at church.

2. Two fields on the east side of Gilberry Gate Lane leading to Bagshaw, formerly Bowden's, are called "Phœnix," and this corresponds with the statement in the Parish Book that the girl was lost on "Bowden's part." She had, therefore, travelled only about a couple of hundred yards before being plunged into the snowdrift. The writer's own experience confirms the ease with which travellers well aquainted with the country can be lost in a blinding Peakland snowstorm.

The observer had seen it several times, "but not so violent as it was these two nights, but could never hear by any what the cause should be."

26 Oct. 1720. John Kenion who was a day labourer and following a London Carrier's horses part of the way from Manchester his master found him on the Moor near Within Lache house very weak and being carried to Within Lache house died there and was buried in the Churchyard the same day.[1]

6 Feb. 1720-1. George Bramwell Sexton of this Church who had been sexton near forty years.

6 Nov. 1727. Hannah d. of Thomas Wilkson, sen. who was going to fetch water and was drowned in a well.

June 1729. "This month there was neither Wedding, Burial, etc."

18 July 1746. Buried S. Hadfield a pauper out of the Workhouse at the Courses.

2 March 1756. Baptism. "James quatuor son of James Shepley Plummer."

N.B. Brass Crossby Esq., Lord Mayor of London and Alderman Oliver put into the Tower, March the 28th 1771.[2]

---

1. This entry shows that the route from Manchester to London via the Midlands passed along the Old Coach Road, up Elnor Lane, and at the back of Ladder Hill; also that the waste land, partly in Chapel and partiy in Fernilee. was still unenclosed.

2. Brass Crossby, an attorney, M.P. for Taunton, and Lord Mayor Nov. 1770, was sent to the Tower by the House of Commons "for dereliction of his duty as M.P." Whilst sitting at the Mansion House he, with other Aldermen, ordered the arrest of a messenger of the House of Commons, who had by its order apprehended in the City of London a printer who had refused to appear at the Bar of the House to answer a charge of having published reports of the proceedings of the House. Crossby had held that the messenger's action was an infringement of the rights of the City. The question as to whether or no the reports of proceedings in Parliament should be published excited great public interest at this time, and it is no doubt on this account that Mr. Byron made the above entry, as Crossby had no connection with Chapel. When the House rose Crossby was released, and no further attempt to interfere with the publication of parliamentary reports has since been made.

N.B. On Sunday, the 14th Sept., 1777, about 11 o'clock in the forenoon (it being a fine day) a smart shock of an Earthquake was felt in this Town and in most parts of the West of England.

At the end of the Second and Third Registers are entries of the baptism of a number of "Bastard Children."

The last pages of No. 3 also contain a transcript of the inscriptions on the Board described in Chapter V, as to the election of Curate with the names of freeholders from time to time co-opted to make up the Twenty-seven.

CHAPTER IX.

PEWS AND BURIALS IN THE CHURCH.

BEFORE the Reformation pews or fixed seats in Parish Churches were the exception and not the rule. Late in the thirteenth century mention of scattered seats in the Nave are to be found, but in 1287 a Synod held by Bishop Quevil of Exeter condemned the allotment of seats to individuals holding that none save "noble persons or patrons" were entitled to claim any seat in the Church. Cases of payments for seats in pre-Reformation times have occurred, as at Salisbury where 6d. per seat was charged and seats allotted, but the legality of such charge was considered doubtful.[1]

As our records only go back to 1620 we have no evidence of the earlier custom within this parish, but entries in the Register prove that by 1661 a more or less vested interest existed in particular pews or seats. With this was bound up a somewhat peculiar system of burial within the Church itself. Of course burial in a place set apart from profane uses and with religious rites has obtained amongst civilised nations for all time, but burial within a church, except in the case of persons of extraordinary merit—of which the incumbent was the judge— was forbidden by Canons of the Church formulated before the time of Edward the Confessor, and it was laid down that there was good reason that any parishioner should not have the liberty of burying there especially on account of the health of the inhabitants assembled for religious worship.[2]

---

1. Gasquet. *Parish Life in Mediæval England.*
2. Phillimore, *Ecclesiastical Law*, 2nd ed., p. 652.

As Chapel Church was erected long after these Canons were passed, it would appear that for some reason not now clear, they were disregarded. References to burial in the Church as far back as the sixteenth century are to be found in the Wills of Thomas Kyrke of Shireoaks in 1548 and of Joan Brockylhurst and her son, all, be it noted, non-parishioners. The old lady's Will is interesting as typical of the pre-Reformation form of Will, having been made in the last year of the reign of Philip and Mary, when the " Old Religion " was still in the ascendant. It runs as follows :—

" In the name of God Amen. the 11th day of Januarii in ye year of our lord god MDLVII (1557/8) Wytenessyth y^t I Jone brockylhurst wyddo of ye pyshe of glossope of gud and perfyte Rememberance make thys my testament and last wylle in manr and forme foloyng ffyrst I bequeath my soule to god the father Almighty whyche hath created yt and to hys only son whyche Redemyd yt and to the holy gost whyche Inspyred yt besekyng our blessed lady saynt mari saynt Mychaell tharchangell and my adwoured saynt so to praye for me and my body to be buried in ye churche of ye Chappell de le fryht and ther to turne to wormys meat.

And thus my soule and body bequeathed I dispose my transytori and worldly good for the health of my soule and quyetnes of my pore chyldren and frynds in manr and forme foloyng fiyrst I bequeath in the nature of my mortuary as ye lawe wyll," etc.

The Will of Oliver Brocklehurst of the Haighe in the parish of Glossop, dated 1st April, 1566, directs that he shall be buried in Chapel-en-le-Frith as near his mother's grave as may be.

The first burial entered in the Register is that of Nicholas Wilson—probably the old husbandman who gave evidence in the case of *Thornhill* v. *Tooker* when he lived in Chinley—who was buried in Church on

PEWS AND BURIALS IN CHURCH

10 December, 1620, followed shortly afterwards by John Olliver of Bugsworth and Richard Ashton of Gorstilow.[1] Burials of total strangers are also recorded from time to time : as an instance there seems no reason why Robert Lambe of Altrincham " who was slaine by a fall from his horse he died in Fernilee " should have been buried in the Chancel on 7th August, 1622, and this is not an isolated case. In the eighteenth century several Incumbents and Parish Clerks were buried in the Chancel.

Written in the list of Parish Officers for the year 1637 is the following :—

"It is agreed by part of the seven and twenty now met this present day being met together that all those out-parishioners who have desire that their friends which shall be buried in our churchyard shall pay unto Mr. Nickson ten grottes and also if it shall be allowed by the Churchwardens to bury in the Church to pay for the said burial the double sum of the leystall whereof the one half to be allowed to the said Minister aforesaid and thus and hereunto we put our hands the XI day of April in the year above written."

Mr. Nickson was the then Minister. It will be observed that the Churchwardens were to allow burials in the Church and in the case of non-parishioners half the "leystall" presumably was to go to them.[2] The term "leystall" is now obsolete, but is believed to refer to a burial place within the Church. It is found in the same connection in the Parish Accounts of Hope and Ashover. The Dictionary definition of the term is a midden or place where refuse is deposited. The fee for "foreign" burials in the Churchyard, according to the

---

1. In the 1702 plan both these families have burial places in the church. The Ashtons may have claimed this as descendants of the family living at Stodhart in the fifteenth and following centuries.
2. "The Churchwardens may also by custom have a fee for every burial in the Church by reason the parish is at the charge of repaving the floor." Phillimore *ubi sup.*

foregoing resolution, would be 3/4 (ten groats) and 6/8 for interments in the Church. At Ashover the leystall was 3/4.

That the Minister and Churchwardens exercised a jurisdiction as to the seats is shown by the following entries in the Register :—

1660-1, Jan. 17th. The Coate of armes belonging to Nicholas Bowden of Bowden[1] in ye countie of Derby Esquire being quartered with ye two coates of his two wifes Woodrofe and Barnby, are placed over the seat belonging to Bowden by consent of us James Hulme,[2]
Henry Kirke }
John Cooper } Churchwardens.

1661, May 25th. A seat was erected in our Chancel of Chappell joyning to ye font for ye Churchwardens to sit in.

1661-2, Feb. 7th. Mem: That it was agreed between Randolph Brown of Marsh and Wm. Barber of Malcoff that the sd. Randolph hath sould one seat or pew next adjoyning to his chief seate or pewe in the Chappell Church, for a valuable consideration in the presence of
James Hulme, Henry Kirke, John Cooper.

1662, Sept. 22. I am contented yt a seat be set upp in ye Chappell Church within St. Nicholas Quyre in ye place adjoynes to Rallph Gee's seat, and belongs to Bings farm and that Francis Gee and Dorothy his wife shall enjoy ye same duringe theire two lives paying all church dues which belongs for ye seat to pay. Nics. Bowden.

---

1. Quarterly *sable* and *or*; in the first quarter a lion passant *arg.*, langued *gu*. These arms may still be seen carved on an old building at Bowden Hall. The crest was an eagle's head erased.
2. James Hulme was the Incumbent.

PEWS AND BURIALS IN CHURCH

Another similar agreement is preserved in the Old Book in the Vestry.

"March 9, 1702. Mem: it is agreed this day between Robt Bagshaw of Dounlee and Henry Kyrk of Chappell that the said Henry Kyrk and his heirs shall quietly occupy and enjoy that part of the said Robt. Bagshaw seat that is in the short forms on the south side in conjunction with Ralph Kyrk to whom the other half of the said form belongs he paying from time to time all such duties and assessments as shall be charged for the same.

                        Robert Bagshaw
                        Henry Kyrke

Robert Middleton   { April 22nd 1708
John Middleton   { I do consent to this agreement above said.
                        Lewis Bagshaw—his mark."

We are indebted to Mr. Ernest Bagshawe, J.P., for permission to reproduce a Map of the Burying Places within and without the Church dated 1709, from the Ford Hall Collection, and to Col. Goodman, C.B., for the following very interesting list of seats from the papers at Eccles House.

ONE SEAT LAY FOR YE RESPECTIVE SEATS IN THE CHURCH.

	s.	d.		s.	d.
Tho: Bagshaw Esqr	10	0	Geo: Thornhill	2	8
Simon Degg Esqr	3	0	Saml. Kirk White-		
Jno Bradshaw Esqr	3	4	haugh	2	8
Robt Bagshaw	2	8	Mr. Buxton	2	8
Geo. Bowdon	2	8	Jno. Bagshaw	2	8
Jno Bennett, White-			Combs Head	2	8
hough Head	2	8	Saml. Kirk fr Cources	2	8
Tho: Bagshaw Esqr	2	8	Slack Hall	2	8
Mr Jno Barber	2	8	Tho. Mellor	2	8

CHAPEL-EN-LE-FRITH PARISH CHURCH

Long Forms in ye South side

Edmd. Warrington	2	0
{ Simon Degg Esqr	2	0
{ Willm Archer Esqr	2	0
{ Willm Middleton	2	0
Slack hall	2	0
Nico. Creswell	2	0
Jam. Carrington	2	0
{ Simon Degg Esqr	1	8
{ Mr Jno Carrington	1	8
{ Jos. Trickett	1	8
Jno. Shirt &c.	4	0
{ Jno. Bennett	1	3
{ Tho. Lomas	1	3
Mr. Flitcroft	1	3
{ Mr Jno Barber	1	3
{ Antho. Bealott	1	3
{ Mr Buxton	1	3
{ Hen : Mellor	1	3
{ Mr Mossley Eaves	1	3
{ Will : Archer Townend	1	8
{ Geo. Ward & Jos. Shirt	1	8
{ Jno. Wild	1	8
{ Geo. Thornhill	3	4
{ Hen : Kirk	1	8
Mr Arnold Kirk	4	8
{ Tho. Cooper	1	8
{ Ralph Hudson Thornilee	1	8
{ Tho : Gee	1	8
{ Nico. Creswell	2	6
{ Hen : Lomas Thornilee	2	6

Long Forms Northside

Tho : Bagshaw Esqr	5	0
{ Hen : Bradshaw Esqr	2	6
{ Jno. Lingard	2	6
{ Fran : Tomason	1	3
{ Mr. Byron pr Oulgreave	1	3
{ James Low	1	3
{ Tho : Cooper	1	3

{ Hurst	1	0
{ Baghouses	2	0
{ Geo : & Saml Kirk	1	0
{ Mr Mossley L	1	8
{ Ralph Hudson		
{ Thornilee	1	8
{ Vid : Mortin Healee	1	8
{ Mr. Jasper Frith	1	8
{ Stephen Bealott	3	4
{ Jno Frith	1	3
{ Combs head	1	3
{ Ralph Dean	1	3
{ Bridgefield	1	3
Mr W. Willm Bagshaw 2 Seats	10	0
{ Jno. Brocklehurst	2	8
{ Adam Young	1	4
{ Geo. Ward	1	8
{ Jno Fletcher	1	8
{ Bet field	1	8
Maglow	3	4
Vid. Sutton	5	8

Above ye Font

Mrs Grace Alleyn &c	3	0
Jno. Gascoign	3	0
Mr Mossley L	2	0
Mr Jno. Carrington	2	0
Mr Scholar	1	0

Behind ye Pulpit

Jam Pickford*		
Ralph Gee	1	4
Simon Degg Esqr	0	8
Jno Goodwin Green	0	4

Ladys Quire South Side

Stephen Bealott	1	4
Jno Lingard Stoddard	1	4
Mr Buxton	1	4
Mr Moult 2 Seats	2	8
Jno. Lingard pr Chapel	1	4
Hall Hill	1	4

PEWS AND BURIALS IN CHURCH

Fran : Tomason	1	4	Mr Mossley L	1	4
Jno Bradshaw Esqr	2	8	Edwd Jackson	1	4
Mr Willm Barber	1	4	Hen : Bagshaw	1	4
Ralph Creswell	1	4	Saml. Kirk & Gee	1	4
Wm Gold 2 Seats	2	8	Robt. Bagshaw	1	4
Richd Dronfield	1	4	Cockyard	1	4
Mr Norton	1	4	Jos. Trickett	1	4
Mr Clows	1	4	New field	1	4
{For Yellot house	0	8	Jno Kirk & Wm Ward	1	4
{Lewis Bagshaw	0	8	Tho. Bennett Light-		
Tho : Kirk & Sam :			birch	1	4
Bagshaw	1	4	Hen : Kirk Pityard	1	4
Diglake	1	4	Richard Turner	1	4
Willm Barber	1	4	*Behind Great Door*		
Hen : Longden & Jno			Mr Moult	1	0
Shirt	1	4	Mr Brown & R. Wain-		
Mrs Waterhouse	1	4	wright	2	0
Mr Clows Laneside &			James Carrington	1	0
Hen : Kirk	1	4	Pyegreave &c	2	0
Geo. Bagshaw &			Peter Wood	1	0
Bullock	1	4	Nic. Redfern Cources	2	0
Geo. Bowdon	1	4	Richd Greensmith	1	4
			Tho. Barber pr Clough	1	4
St. Nicholas Quire			Hen : Marchington	1	0
Peter Wood	1	4			
Hen : Kirk Eaves	1	4	*Chancell*		
Jno. Bennett Silkhill	1	4	Robt Middleton	1	0
Mr Barber	1	4	Geo. Ward[1]	1	0
Mr Creswell	1	4	Stephen Bellott &		
Saml. Frith	1	4	Matt : Walker	1	0
Jno. Shirt	1	4			
Wilkin hill	1	4	Total ... 13	1	4
Nic. Kirk Laneside	1	4			

The plan, which it will be noticed, was copied in 1747 from an older one dated 1709, is of great interest. It was apparently prepared under the instructions of George Bramal, the Sexton, an office still held by a member of

---

1. "Apl. 18, 1693. Geo : Ward has a pew in the Chancell, has paid 12d. per lay for the said pew. John Kirke and Edward Shirte churchwardens. Wm. White minister.'. Note in P.R.

his family, and sundry notes, such as the allowance of the Yeaveley burying place to Mr. Frith by the Rev. B. Bardsley, show that it was brought up to date.

It is further interesting as indicating the position of the Pulpit, the Bowden Tomb and the old Steeple, the latter being shown at the west end of the North Aisle and not on the site of the present tower.

Also it will be observed that the only entrance to the Church shown on the plan adjoins the steeple, no south door to the Church or Chancel appearing. The long vacant strip approaching the steeple no doubt was the site of the footpath leading to it, and the similar broader strip on the south side would reach the Church at the point where there would probably be a doorway not shown in the plan where the present south porch was erected in 1733. It is difficult to determine with precision boundaries between the Church and Churchyard or the internal arrangement of the Church, as the plan does not appear to be drawn to any scale, but with the assistance of some gravestones still *in situ*—such as that of Needham of Perry near the east end of the south aisle and that of Thomas Moult of Tunstead Milton to the south-west of the present tower—we can obtain a rough idea. This plan and the assessment list in conjunction with the plan of the allotment of seats on the re-pewing in 1834, throw considerable light on the connection of the pews or seats with the burying places and on the continuity of occupation of the seats by successive owners and occupiers of the same dwelling house.

The seat lay list states the assessment for the whole Church to be £13 1s. 4d., which total corresponds exactly with the Churchwardens seat lay total in their account for 1717. This list is particularly valuable as it contains the only reference to "Ladys Quire South side" that we have met with between the reign of Philip and Mary and the present day.

A comparison of the 1709 plan with the 1728 List and

the allotment of 1834 demonstrates that in many, but not by any means all, cases the seat or pew was immediately over or in close proximity to the family burial place, and to some extent the allotment of 1834 was on similar lines—the Award, indeed, stating that the seats allotted were as near their former situation as circumstances would permit.

The Rev. Samuel Pegge, the antiquarian Rector of Whittington, when he visited the Church in the latter part of the eighteenth century, remarked " 'tis miserably pewed," but it was not until 1818 that any steps were taken to provide new seats. In that year it was decided to re-pew the body of the Church. Shortly afterwards the Rev. R. R. Rawlins mentions that the Church contained some old carved pews with dates cut on them varying from 1621 to 1710. From local sources we have learned that some of these pews were gorgeously upholstered in red velvet and gold, etc., whilst others had canopies—the floor was strewn with rushes which, when they dried, crackled as numbers of mice ran about to the real or assumed terror of the female worshippers. When the floor was relaid the surface beneath is said to have been covered with bones. An examination of the base of the piers indicates that the present floor of the nave is about 13 inches above its original level. There were also at this time galleries at the east end of the Chancel and the west end of the Church. Although the re-pewing was decided upon in 1818 it was sixteen years before the work was finally completed. In the meantime a rather large scheme of rebuilding the Chancel and the east end of the Church had been discussed and finally abandoned, probably from lack of funds. In 1825 the Vestry came to the conclusion that many of the seats were "entirely rotten and in a very bad state of repair." This contemporary statement is some reply to Dr. Cox' rather sweeping criticism of the conduct of our ancestors in this and other matters connected with the Church.¹ Much new information has come to light, however, since he wrote.

Eventually the body of the Church was re-pewed as it is to this day—the seats in the Chancel were similar in form but faced the west,² and so remained until 1892. Since the last-mentioned date the seating accommodation is officially stated to be 750. A Faculty for repewing was granted under the Seal of the Dean and Chapter of Lichfield in 1827 and five Commissioners, the Incumbents of Fairfield, Castleton and Taxal with Mr. G. W. Newton of Taxal and John White, Esq., of Park Hall, were thereby appointed Commissioners to make the Allotment, which was carried out in 1834. The cost, £500, was raised by public subscription, and the "Gentlemen of the Committee" were Walter Joseph Gisborne, Esq., Thomas Goodman, Esq., John Bennett, James Hibberson, Adam Fox, of Martinside, Joseph Storer, John Ibbotson, and William Yates. Some of the seat-holders took possession of the old oak forming these seats and converted them into cupboards, etc., which are still to be found in the farmhouses of the Parish. The then Vicar of Buxton, the Rev. and Hon. Francis Grey, begged two cart loads of pew ends, etc., which are now incorporated with the panelling in St. Ann's Church, Higher Buxton.

To many of the new pews was attached a neat brass plate with the name of the house or property to which the seats had been allotted, and these remained in position until removed in 1894 by the Churchwardens on the advice of the Chancellor of the Diocese, Mr. A. B. Kempe, Q.C. Some of these plates, of ornate design, are now preserved in the vestry.

A story that we fear is well founded is that during the

---

1. *Churches of Derbyshire*, ii., *passim*.
2. It is said that a similar arrangement of seats was to be found in another church, Symondsbury, Dorset. *Treasury Magazine*, Jan., 1917.

PEWS AND BURIALS IN CHURCH

alterations the Font was temporarily placed in the Churchyard, and that a local lawyer being unable to obtain payment of his charges and disbursements for obtaining the Faculty, took possession of the Font, with the acquiescence of the Wardens—and placed it in his garden. The Rev. Mr. Grey would have liked the Font as well as the old oak, but Mr. . . . . . said it must not go out of the Parish. Ultimately, after some years, by the good offices of the late Mr. Needham of Rushop, the Font was restored to its rightful place in the Church. Whilst the Font was out of the Church a small basin—fixed in the south angle of the Communion rails—was used; this remained *in situ* until the present Altar rails were erected.

CHAPTER X.

THE BELLS AND RINGERS.

WE do not know when the Church was first provided with bells but that it had at least one for many years prior to 1701 is shown by a note made in the Register for that year by James Pickford, the Parish Clerk:—

"The great Bell now in our Steple was taken down to be cast upon Friday, the 27th day of June, 1701, and as it was coming down the pullis broak and the bell fell to the ground and broke two beams of the lower floor and brought all before it. The man who was above to guide it was Ezekiell Shutleworth a Joyner in this town, but seeing the pullis break could noways help himself but came after it a lader with him and a little crow of iron in his hand and yet the man by God's great preservation had little or no harm.

I James Pickford present Clarke was at the rope in the Church when it fell.

The great Bell was cast at Wigan August the 6 1701. Mr. German Buxton and George Thornhill were Churchwardens that year. I James Pickford went with Mr. Buxton to see it cast. Mr. William Scott was the founder and was Alderman of Wigan that year."

It does not follow that because the Great Bell is spoken of there were other bells in the steeple.

W have not been able to trace any report of the Church Goods Commissioners 6 Edward VI (1553) as to this parish, but at that time many Derbyshire Churches had from one to three "Great Bells" and a "Little" or Sacring Bell, and in some places handbells. It therefore seems likely that Chapel had only one bell in the steeple at this time and a small or Sanctus Bell in the bell-cote above the Chancel Arch.[1] The present bell-cote, being in the Georgian style, obviously takes the place of an older one replaced by the restorers of 1733 without any understanding of its import. It was said thirty years ago that long after 1733 there was a bell in this small chamber, there being distinct marks of the bell-stay and the friction of the chain in the Chancel, and a story was told of this bell having at some period been removed to Bowden Hall its subsequent history being unknown, but it is believed to have been worn out and ultimately destroyed some years ago.

When the present tower was built in 1733, six bells were hung. Five at least of these were cast at Gloucester by the famous bell founder, Abraham Rudhall, whose business is still carried on by Messrs. Mears and Stainbank of Whitechapel, London. Enquiry was made of the latter some years ago as to whether this was a new peal or was re-cast, but their records do not show this. The marks, etc., on the bells are as follows:—

		Weight cwt.	Note
Treble.	"Peace and good neighbourhood"	$4\frac{3}{4}$	E
2nd.	"Prosperity to this Parish" ...	5	D
3rd.	"We were all cast at Glocester by A. Rudhal, 1733"	6	C
4th.	No inscription or date	7	B
5th.	"Jasper Frith and John Wainwright, Churchwardens" ...	8	A
Tenor.	"I to the Church the living call And to the Grave do summon all 1733"	11	G

---

1. Cresswell's petition in 1617 speaks of "bells," this may, however have been merely a legal formula. See p. 63.

The Treble, 2nd and 5th bells bear the mark of Abraham Rudhall—a bell between the initials A. R.—and the date 1733. The inscriptions are in Roman Capital letters, in one line round the haunches of the bells. Treble, 2nd, 3rd and 5th have a border of a *fleur de lys* pattern.

It has been suggested that as No. 4 is not dated or inscribed like the other bells it is the " Great Bell " recast in 1701.

The cost of these bells and of the general restoration of the Church at this time was to be defrayed, in part at least, by Briefs, but the full account of the receipts and payments has disappeared and there is no record of how they were met beyond the sum of £50 paid to the Builder in 1732, which must have come out of the " land-leys."

Sundry items with reference to the new peal will be found in the Churchwardens' Accounts, from which it appears that the work was undertaken in 1731, and " articles " with Mr. Rudhall are referred to in the following year, the last payment being discharged on 22nd August, 1734, on which occasion 1/6 was spent.

The Wardens' Accounts show that if the bells were rung on Sundays the ringers had no regular payment for this service until 1754 when they received 3/- for ringing before service on Sunday, and the account for 1757 makes it quite clear that they only received 4/- " for the year for 2 peals each Sunday." This seems a remarkably inadequate remuneration, but throughout the greater part of the eighteenth century, as the accounts show, the ringers received numerous sums varying from 3/- to 12/- for ringing on Guy Fawkes' Day and in celebration of Victories, interesting events in the lives of the Royal Family, and so on, not forgetting peals on Fast Days and Good Friday. In fact the Belfry was something like the contents bill of a modern newspaper : an invitation to the parishioners to enquire " what's the news ? "

In 1767, however, the Wardens " by agreement of the parishioners," paid £2 a year, and by 1778 the ringers had £3 per annum whilst they were still paid for ringing on special occasions. The Peak Forest ringers were here on two successive Sundays and had 2/6 on each occasion. This was the great year in which the organ was installed, and the Wardens' account contains the curious item " paid to Mr. John Pickford towards ye organist's salary in lieu of a Rushbearing and 3 Holy Days took from the ringers £2. 5. 0."

Like some other arts that of campanology often has a strong hereditary appeal, and we see in at least one local family cogent proof of this rule.

The Fords have been ringers for some five generations and can claim well over a century's service to the church. The late Mr. George Ford, of Woodbine Cottage, who died in 1920, had a record of 68 years' ringing to his credit, and he had also the unique experience of ringing in peals celebrating the Declarations of Peace after the Crimean War in 1856, the Boer War in 1900, and the Great War in 1918—on the last occasion with a son-in-law and grandson in the " team." Mr. Ford's grandfather, father, uncle, son and nephew were all ringers at one time or another, and a well-founded tradition in the family is that in the latter part of the eighteenth century his great grandfather also had a place in the Belfry. Mr. James Ford, a brother of George, sang in the choir for over half a century, and yet another relative, Mr. John Ford, was for many years a scripture reader.

Another family who may almost be said to live in the Belfry are the Hibberts, one of whom now rings the daily bells on Sundays and week days.

From an old undated record we find that more than a century ago the bells were specially rung on the Anniversary of the Martyrdom of King Charles I, 30th January, the bells being muffled on one side and the ringing commencing the evening before.

The Restoration of Charles II, 29th May, when it was the ringers' duty to adorn the Church tower and porch with branches of oak.[1]

The Birthday of George III.

The 5th November and the evening before when the ringers had 15/- and a goose at the Bull's Head, and New Year's Eve to ring the Old Year out and the New Year in, this last being still observed.

Some old customs are still happily kept up and the following single bells are rung:—

Sundays, at 8 a.m. and 1 p.m.,[2] the first and second bells are rung together.

One bell at 12 noon (11 o'clock on Shrove Tuesday) on week days.

The Curfew at 8 p.m. on every week-night, except Saturday, when it is rung at 7 o'clock.

One bell is first rung for a few minutes and the 4th bell then is tolled to give the day of the month.

The "Passing Bell," according to a custom that appears to be dying out, was rung for any person dying in the town (*i.e.*, on the Church side of Smithy Brook) immediately after the death, but never before 8 a.m.; for any other person on the morning of the funeral before 8 a.m., the time of ringing and the number of strokes thus giving the listeners some information about the deceased. For a girl under 16 each bell is tolled 3 times, for a boy under 16, 4 times, for a woman over 16, 5 times, and for a man over 16, 7 times, in each case followed by the Tenor bell for half an hour.

---

1. A similar custom is still preserved in the neighbouring parish of Castleton, where a great wreath is attached to the tower on 29th May (Garland Day).

2. It is said that these bells were rung to remind people to get ready for church in times when there was no peal. We are, however, inclined to think that they had their origin in the summons to pre-Reformation services. We know of one Roman Catholic place of worship where a bell is rung at 1 p.m. on Sundays.

CHAPTER XI.

MUSIC AND SINGING.

OUR knowledge of the musical side of the Church Services before the middle of the eighteenth century is reduced to such as we can glean from the Wardens' Accounts. That there was a " loft for the Psalm Singers " at the west end of the Church, which had been there for a long period, is shown in the Faculty of 1754 to which we shall presently refer.

From 1748 onwards we find numerous items in the Accounts from which we select the following :—

1748 Apl. 25		Spent on the Singers with ye Freeholders consent	8	0
1749 May 21		Spent with the Peak Forest Singers	2	6
	June 11	Spent upon Eyam Singers	2	6
	Feby	Given to the Singers	6	0
1750	Dec.	Spent upon the singers	8	0
1752		Spent upon the singers	5	0
1752		Paid for repairing the Bassoon for singers	8	0
1759		Paid for a crane for the Bassoon for singers	2	6
1760		Gave to Mottram Singers	5	0
1761	Feb.	Gave the singers a treat	6	0
	May	Gave Disley Singers in ale	5	0
1763	May	Sent Hope Singers their treat being omitted when they came here	5	0
1766		Paid for two Bassoon Reeds for Singers	2	0

1770	Spent at proving the Bass Violin	4	0
1772	Paid for two Bass Violin Strings and other repairs	1	4
1774	Paid Isaac Watts for the Bassoon ordered two years since	18	6
	John Frith for Hautboy Reed and case	5	0
1773	Given to Singers of Edall	5	0
1780	Spent upon Hayfield Singers	7	6
	Spent at Wm. Potts upon Singers	5	0
1783 July 13	Given to Tideswell singers	5	0

The last date suggests that some of the visits of neighbouring singers were at Wakes time or, as in 1803, at the "School Sermons." The records of neighbouring parishes would no doubt show that such visits were interchangeable.

About the year 1754 Mr. Byron, the then Vicar, obtained a Faculty to erect a gallery over the Nave and South Aisle—the seats over the Nave being let to parishioners and those over the South Aisle being for the use of the "Psalm Singers," whose older loft was to be replaced by the new scheme.

So things went on for nearly a quarter of a century, till in 1777, "encouraged by the firm support of a few generous individuals who wish well to the House of God and the Honour of the Christian Religion," an appeal was made to the parishioners setting forth that "an earnest desire of having an Organ erected in the Parish Church of Chapel-en-le-Frith hath long prevailed among the major part of the parishioners, but through a want of activity on the one hand, and the fear of expense on the other, no vigorous attempts have hitherto been made in the prosecution of so laudable a design." Subscriptions were solicited and the inevitable Committee was formed, comprising Mr. Byron (Treasurer), George

Goodman and Samuel Frith, Esqs., the Rev. John Gee,[1] James Carrington, Gent., Cornelius Pickford, Thomas Hudson, William Yates, and others.

There was a generous response, £263 7s. 9d. being quickly given by 133 subscribers of £20 (each by Mr. Goodman and Mr. Frith) down to 2/6 (with "odd subscriptions" £1 7s. 6d.). A full list of donors is preserved in the Church safe and includes eight subscribers of 5/3 each, presumably "quarter guinea."[2] The Committee were granted a Faculty to erect a gallery under or near the Great Arch leading out of the Chancel into the body of the Church with steps or stairs out of the Chancel on the south side and to place an organ in this gallery with eight seats or pews besides a seat in front for the organist and another behind for the bellows-blower, and to build six new seats or pews in the gallery at the west end, extending the gallery to the north end of the Church. The Committee were to let the seats in the organ loft and in the new part of the west gallery, and to pay an organist out of rents to play the organ on Sundays and other days during Divine Service.

The tender of Mr. Richard Parker of Manchester which was accepted was "to make an organ of one sett and half of keys from double gamutt long eights to D. in alt. inclusive, 55 in number, and to these keys the following stops: An open Diapason of metal down to gamutt and the rest stopt pipes of wood below." Then follows a list of 469 "speaking pipes" in great organ and 575 in swell organ. "This organ will answer two setts and a half of keys." The whole to be furnished with two pair of bellows in a workmanlike manner with all things thereto belonging, the case to be of oak with a deal back for £150: the contractor to find packing cases having

---

1. Of the Lydgate family, a former rector of Taxal and then, we believe, residing at Chestnut House.
2, *Cf. The Rivals*, act ii., sc. ii. Sir Anthony Absolute: "I'll lodge a five-and-threepence in the hands of Trustees."

them returned, and the Committee to pay carriage. A seven years warranty was given, "fire, water, violence and vermin excepted."

Edward Bennett tendered for the erection of the gallery at £29 10s., but the contract was let to Daniel Armstrong and Thomas Bagshaw, whose tender is not preserved. Their bill, however, is interesting as showing that the pay of masters and men was alike, 1/8 per day.

The galleries and organ being completed in the early summer of 1778, so great an occasion was fitly celebrated on July 13th and 14th (which would be Monday and Tuesday in Wakes Week) by the performance in the Parish Church of two oratorios: *The Messiah*, then in the first flush of its fame, and *Judas Maccabeus*.

The following account of the payments and receipts shows the importance of this interesting and unique performance. The fees paid were *Violins*, Mr. Jobson £12 12s. od., Mr. Garner £3 3s. od., Mr. Garner, Jun., and Mr. Marshall each £2 2s. od. *Hautboys*, Mr. Hutchinson and Mr. Shepley each £3 3s. od. *Trumpets and Horns*, Mr. Hague £5 5s. od., Mr. Lucas £2 2s. od. *'Cello*, Mr. Hague, Mr. Wood, Sen., £1 1s. od. *Bassoons*, Mr. Whitehead and Mr. Clough each £2 2s. od. *Drums and Clarinets*, Mr. Marsey £2 12s. 6d. *Organ*, Mr. Buckley £5 5s. od. *Treble*, Miss Barnes £5 5s. od., Miss Harwood £3 3s. od., Mrs. Field and Mrs. Beaumont £1 11s. 6d. each. *Counter*, Mr. W. Nield £2 2s., Messrs. Heywood, sen. and jun., £1 11s. 6d. *Tenor*, Messrs. Ogden, Haughton and Davis £2 2s. od each, Mr. Walker £1 11s. 6d. *Bass*, Mr. Jas Nield £3 3s. od., Mr. Radcliffe £2 2s. od., Messrs. Hague and Shaw £1 11s. 6d. each, Mr. Parkes £1 1s. od. *Temporary Stage*, £1 2s. od. *Tickets*, £3 10s. od. Total payments £85 9s. od. 300 Gallery Tickets at 2/6, 700 Church Tickets at 1/-, and 100 books (price not stated) were issued each day to Mr. Orgill and Mrs. Slack, " Gallery Tickett " was given to Mrs. Orgill and another to Mrs.

Slack, while the Constable (2), Churchwardens (4), Clerk and Sexton (4), and R. Middleton (1) were presented with Church Tickets. A pathetic little note at the end of the account adds: "These oratorios lost £19 5s. 6d., that is to say the above in the whole."

Not only was this loss incurred, but the performance of such works in the Church aroused violent anger in the breasts of some of the parishioners as may be gathered from the following "verses," said to have been posted on the Church gates about this time. These were copied many years ago from a long screed of 61 lines in the possession of an old parishioner, long since dead, whose family was closely connected with parochial matters in the eighteenth and nineteenth centuries.

"To the Churchwardens of Chapel en le Frith and others whom it may concern.

> In Bowden Chapel not long since
> Where Satan sometimes rules as Prince,
> A Church was built to worship in,
> There did the devil wars begin:
> The Protestant and Schismatick
> Fell out about a Candlestick.
> The Father, Sister, Son and Brother,
> Fought till they'd ruined one another.
> And then the Church had rest awhile
> Till strolling Fiddlers did defile
> The place, and Heaven and Earth affront,
> By making a vile play house on't.
> And now each Day as Story tells,
> They scold and brawl about the Bells.
> The D . . . l and one Mr. Yates[1]
> A man who all religion hates
> This year is hir'd to be Ch . . . . w . . . . n,
> Tho' he's much fitter for Bear Garden.

---

1. William Yates was warden in 1781.

Where's Coventry and Lichfield's grace
They visit not this wicked place
Would Bishops excommunicate
Churchwardens who are profligate
It would be good for Church and State,
Rise B . . . n[1] from thy easy chair
And mount the pulpit to declare
The curses which attend on those
Who laws of God and men oppose,
And let Y . . . s know he's not the keys
O'th Church to do whate'er he please."

The provision of an organ naturally required the appointment of an organist, and on 8th February, 1778, the Vestry resolved " To take off the money given to the Overseers of the Highways in Bradshaw, Bowden and Combs Edge and the same along with what was usually allowed for a Rush Cart be appropriated as an addition to the Salary of an organist," and the Freeholders present " unanimously consented to the same in order to avoid any additional expense coming upon the Parish." In the Churchwardens' Accounts for this year is the item " Paid to Mr. John Pickford towards ye Organist's salary in lieu of a Rushbearing and 3 Holy Days took from the Ringers £2 5s. od."

The resolution as to the money given to the Overseers is rather cryptic, presumably it was an honorarium voted to them as " expenses," but the justice of thus mulcting them in favour of the organist is not now quite apparent.

Items similar to those quoted occur in subsequent accounts well into the nineteenth century. In 1805 is a payment of 12/- to the ringers and singers " being

---

1. Evidently the vicar, the Rev. John Byron, then an old man. The reference to his easy chair probably had a point that we cannot now appreciate.

Christmas Day," but in the following year 6/- only was paid to the singers.

We have been unable to find any record of the erection of the gallery in the Chancel, but it has been spoken of by several old people, and appears to have been removed when the Church was re-pewed about 1830. It is said to have stood in front of the Altar and was reached by a stair on the south side close to the present door. In it was a small organ described as "like a box organ," worked by a handle like a barrel organ, with seats for the musicians in front. A famous player of those days was one Abraham Lomas, a barber of Townend, who sat in front of the organ and performed on the Bass Viol; he also played an instrument known as a Serpent in the Band, and in addition was a noted singer. At that time Mr. William Barber, the father of the late Mr. Henry Barber, J.P., of New Mills, was the organist, and at his death in December, 1865, had held the office for no less than 49 years. Mr. Thomas D. Goodman took his place and was succeeded by Mr. Edwin Walker, who officiated for 45 years.

Mr. Henry Barber was also a musician, and as an old poster testifies presided at the organ on Sunday, 24th September, 1865, when two sermons were preached by the Rev. George Hall, the Vicar, and collections were "made for the encouragement of the Choir of the above Church." Handel again figures largely in the "Selection of Sacred Music sung on the occasion," and it is interesting to observe that Evensong still took place at "a quarter before three in the afternoon."

A Tideswell worthy, Mr. Slack, a magnificent Bass Singer, was a frequent and honoured helper in the Singers' loft. He had a remarkably fine ear, and it is told of him that on one occasion when the Chapel and Tideswell ringers were ringing changes at our Church Mr. Slack walked over from Tideswell to the top of Peaslows to listen to the bells. He remarked to his friends that his son, who rang the tenor bell, was ringing badly and throwing the others out, and on their return the Tideswell ringers confirmed this.

In those days many young women worked in the mills at Glossop and would walk home on Saturday evenings, some of them sang in the Choir on Sundays, and after service (then held in the afternoon) would walk back to Glossop singing as they went.

After the East Gallery was demolished the Choir and Organ returned to the West Gallery, where they were located till it was taken down in 1894.

For more than a century the " School Sermons " have been a great day for Choir and Congregation alike. Some of the hymn papers for these services have been preserved in the Vestry. Thus on Sunday, 28th August, 1803, when the preacher was the Rev. L. Heapy of Macclesfield, Handel was, as in 1778, much in evidence, the programme including "Comfort ye," "Every Valley," and the "Hallelujah Chorus." A year or two later we have another sheet announcing a "Charity Sermon " to be preached by the Rev. Mr. Shipley, Vicar of Ashbourne (1806—1850), on Sunday, 11th October, at 2.30 p.m., for the benefit of the Sunday School, "when a collection will be made for that excellent institution." Then follow the hymns which are to be sung by the scholars and the principal singers from the neighbouring places. Before the service is to be sung an Ode commencing :—

> " Blest be the man whose lib'ral heart,
> Our Sunday Schools began;
> To train the youth in virtue's path,
> How God-like was the plan."

An anthem from the 41st Psalm, " Blessed is he that considereth the poor and needy," is " to be sung in the Anthem's place."

MUSIC AND SINGING

The notice which, by the way, is printed in Macclesfield, concludes: "The Organ, which hath just been cleaned and tuned will be played by Mr. Simms, Organist from Ashbourne." (Messrs. Simms received £10 10s. 0d. in 1801 for repairing and tuning the organ.) In 1803 Robert Marshall was the organist, and succeeding him for several years was John Marshall at a salary of £14 per annum.

Amongst the undoubted improvements effected in 1894 was the total demolition of the west gallery, the construction of the present organ chamber opening from the Chancel at the east end of the south aisle, and the removal of the Choir to the Chancel, the system of a "mixed" choir of male and female voices being still preserved. For most of this work the Church was indebted to the late Mr. Samuel Needham of Lower Eaves.

CHAPTER XII.

MISCELLANEA.

USE OF THE CHURCH FOR SECULAR PURPOSES.

IN pre-Reformation days we find many records of the use of Churches in Derbyshire and elsewhere for various secular purposes, but with the coming of the Reformation such use became exceedingly rare. There are, however, several proofs that Chapel Church was so utilised in the sixteenth and seventeenth centuries. It will be remembered that in the depositions in the case of *Thornhill* v. *Tooker,* Nicholas Wilson relates how when the emissary of the Countess of Shrewsbury and the Dean of Lichfield came in Elizabethan times to claim the vacant incumbancy " the parishioners or the most part of them went into the Chancel of the said Church and conferred together," and in 1778 the holding of a Vestry meeting with reference to the organist's salary was held in the Chancel *on a Sunday*—apparently as a matter of course.

That the Church was used for more purely secular purposes is shown by the following document :—

" By virtue of Her Majesty's Commission out of her Highnesses most honourable Court of Chancery to us and others directed for the examination of witnesses touchinge a certain cause in the said Court dependinge betweene Thomas Wright, Plaintiff, and Richard Harford and William Redfearne defendants. These shall be to wyll and require you and everie of you whose names are wrytten in the list in Her Majesty's name most stryghtly to charge and command that you fail not to appear before us and other of our assessors in the church of the Chappell in the Frithe in the County of Derbye upon the Saturday the 8th day of the instant June, by nyne of the clocke in the forenoon there to speak and declare your knowledge touchinge such matters as shall be laid before you.

Given under our hands and seals 7th day of June, 1591.

Roger Columbell
Henry Bagshawe.

To Agnes Kirke, Richard Bouden, Thomas Mellor, etc., etc.[1]

In the early part of the seventeenth century the Chancel was used as a Schoolroom; the President of the Chapter writing to the inhabitants within the Parish of Chapel-en-le-Frith, says :—

"I dare presume so farr in their (the Dean and Chapter) absence not dowting of their contentment to give license and liberty for your schoolmaster to heare his schollares in the Chancell provided that you keepe and leave the same in good and sufficient repaire at youre owne cost and charge according to your promise under your hands."

The Register under date Sept. 11, 1648, records a more extraordinary use of the Church as a temporary prison for a portion of the Scottish Army taken after their defeat by the soldiers of the Commonwealth :—

" There came to this town of Scots army led by the Duke of Hambleton (Hamilton) and squandered by Colonell Lord Cromwell sent hither prisoners from Stopford (Stockport) under the conduct of Marshall Edward Matthews said to be 1500 in number, put into

---

1. *Reliquary*, vol. 9, p. 20.

ye church Sep. 14. They went away Sep. 30 following. There were buried of them before the rest went away 44 persons, and more buried Oct. 2 who were not able to march, and the same y^t died by the way before they came to Cheshire 10 and more."[1]

There is a tradition at Derwent that certain Scotch rebels of "the '45" were imprisoned and starved to death in the old Chapel. It seems much more likely that these were a section of the Scottish prisoners of 1648, like those at Chapel, quartered in the Church for the time being.

As late as 1836 the Poll for the election of an incumbent was held in the Vestry and the result declared in the Chancel.

Recusants and Quakers.

Under the various Acts of Uniformity and Supremacy it was the duty of the Parish Constables and other officials to report to Quarter Sessions the names of those who did not attend their Parish Church, and from 1575 onwards this duty seems to have been zealously performed.

In 1591 a secret report on the action of Gilbert Talbot, Earl of Shrewsbury, presented to the Privy Council by Robert Bainbridge of Derby, one of the County Coroners, mentions that the Earl had appointed John Tunstead (of Tunstead, Wormhill), Bailiff of the High Peak, an office of much "creditt thear by reason that few Justices doo inhabitt y^t wyld country," in which Hundred it is estimated there are near 400 recusants

---

[1] In the summer of 1648 a Scottish Army under the Duke of Hamilton entered England and fought its way through Lancashire to Warrington. Here, after a loss of 1,000 men and 2,000 prisoners, General Bayley, commanding the Infantry, surrendered his whole force. Hamilton and the Horse fled towards Nantwich. 500 being taken on the way by the country people, and himself surrendered at Uttoxeter to the Parliamentary forces. *The Civil Warre in Great Britain and Ireland, ubi sup.*

"of one sorte and other." Tunstead's brother is suspected of being concerned in the Babington conspiracy. The report further states that this John hath also placed known and dangerous recusants to be his under-bailiff as, namely, George Bagshaw of Marsh Green[1] in Chapel Parish which George hath a sister, one widow Mellors, "a most obstinate recusant and greatly suspected by those y^t favor the state."

The Bagshaws of Marsh Green, now extinct in the male line, were for many generations ardent adherents of the "Old Religion" to which so many in the High Peak remained faithful long after the Reformation. Robert Bagshawe of Marsh Green, who was educated at Tideswell Grammar School, was from 1581 to 1589 at the famous Roman Catholic College at Douay in France.

Three of these Bagshaws, Oliver, Dorothy and William, are reported as recusants in 40 Elizabeth, and six persons of the same name, Henry, Florence his wife, Thomas, Agneta, Radus and William were indicted at the Lent Assizes at Derby, in 1616, as also were Margaret, Johanna, Henry and Thomas Mellor, Dorothy Ridge, Agnes Wright and John Morten, also Jane, wife of Henry Mellor, John Mellor and Maria Ridge. At the Summer Assizes three years later Richard Beightowe, Anna Kyrk, Jane Mellor and Gertrude, wife of Thomas Yellott, were likewise indicted.[2]

In 1634, George Thornhill, Constable of Bowden Chapel, presented the following "popish Recusants" for absence from Church for one month last past : Henry Mellor of Tunstead, yeoman, and Jane his wife; George Swindell the elder, of Chapel, husbandman, and his wife; Francis Taylor of Marsh Green, Carpenter, and his wife; George Clarke of Ridge, labourer; Robert Bag-

---

1. He is described as of Hollin Knowle in a MS. Pedigree in the possession of the late Mr. Joseph Heathcott, J.P.
2. *Derbys. Arch. Soc. Journ.*, vol. 16, p. 140.

shawe of Hollin Knowle, yeoman, and Arnold Kirke of Martinside, yeoman.[1]

In 1677, the Bishops, alarmed at the recusancy of the Duke of York, obtained returns from the clergy as to the religious views of the people. The return for Chapel parish gives 587 Conformists, 3 Papists and 8 Nonconformists over the age of 16 years. From this return we may roughly calculate the population of the parish to have been from 900 to 1,000.

At Derby Assizes in August, 1682, five persons are returned as recusants, John and Margaret Lingard and William Beard (Quakers), and Thomas and Henry Kirke and the two first-named with Elizabeth Lingard are again returned as Quakers in 1689. There was a colony of Quakers at Slack Hall at this time, one of whom, Jonathan Bowden, was fined £20 for preaching there and 5/- for attending the same conventicle.

Some Eighteenth Century Litigation.

It is rather curious that whilst the parishioners held firmly together when their right of patronage was challenged, both in the seventeenth and eighteenth centuries, and whilst in the latter century they must have provided very handsome sums for the heavy expenses incurred in re-casting the Great Bell, providing a new peal and the reconstruction of so much of the Church, and again later on, their new organ, there was during much of this period a strong party who were, to say the least of it, decidedly unfriendly to the Minister and Churchwardens. The explanation for this may lie in the

---

1. Henry Mellor of Tunstead, in Chapel Parish, was probably the son of Widow Mellors, mentioned above. It is doubtful if Arnold Kirke were a papist, as less than seventy years later the Kirkes of Martinside were strong supporters of the Apostle of the Peak and Dr. Clegg. The Constable probably classed all non-church-goers as "Papists." It may, therefore, be wise to accept these classifications with some degree of caution. The 1677 return emphasises this. There must have been at that time cons;derably more than eight nonconformist families in the parish, although they might outwardly conform.

slightly strained relations between the Churchmen and the adherents of Chinley Chapel, for Dr. Clegg is usually on the side of the opposition, and most of the other malcontents were members of his congregation.

The Doctor's real Christian character, however, did not permit him to be often at variance with individuals for any length of time, and it is clear that the action of himself and his friends was actuated by what they believed to be their public duty rather than by mere personal pique. When we consider some of the "pin-pricks" to which Stuart and Georgian nonconformists were subject, we can hardly wonder at their attitude. On more than one occasion exuberant young people alleged (probably incorrectly) to be adherents of the church, made disturbances and even committed damage at the chapel, but about this period the wardens seem to have indulged in a mild persecution. They issued a citation in the Ecclesiastical Court against Clegg for non-payment of his Church assessments, and although he tendered the amount, £3 13s. od., twice to John Wainwright, one of the Wardens, "at ye sign of the Roebuck" where Wainwright apparently lived, he complained that it was refused.[1] The Wardens afterwards tried to compel Dr. Clegg to take an apprentice, apparently on the ground that he was a farmer, which in itself was quite correct, but it was looked upon by him as a studied insult and a refusal to acknowledge him as a minister of religion. The Doctor, however, was not taking this "lying down," and when the local Justices approved the Churchwardens' action he appealed to Quarter Sessions at Bakewell and " after a brisk trial " won his case.

---

1. It is not clear whether this was the present Roebuck Inn. In the Gisborne Deeds of 1740 the premises are called "the New Hall," and there is no suggestion that it was then an Inn. It was once the "town-house" of the Shallcross family, and previous to that belonged to the Yeaveleys.

Some years before this there had been some disputes between the freeholders and the trustees of Mr. Wm. Barber of Malcalf, the brother-in-law of the Apostle of the Peak. Mr. Barber left a sum of money for pious and charitable purposes, and for many years part of it had been paid to a "protestant dissenting minister residing and officiating in the parish," *i.e.*, the Apostle while he lived, and the remainder to the poor of the parish. The freeholders, disapproving of this, Mr. Thomas Bagshawe of Bakewell, "who was by far the largest freeholder in the said Parish," was asked to arbitrate, and he proposed that " 20/- should be paid to the Incumbent of Chapel and 20/- to a Protestant Dissenting Minister inhabiting in the said parish, and the remainder to the poor of Chapel," and this was agreed to in December, 1726. But two years later a Commission enquiring into Derbyshire Charities decided that one-third of the income must be paid to the Incumbent and two-thirds to the poor. Mr. Bagshawe of Ford, however, continued to pay 15/- per annum to " Master James Clegg," as he is styled in a bond given to Mr. Bagshawe in 1750, to indemnify him against any claim made by aggrieved parishioners, and it is pleasing to see that amongst the bondsmen were the Incumbent, Mr. Byron, and Mr. Jasper Frith, which shows that by this time a kindlier spirit prevailed, aided, perhaps, as the eulogy in the Parish Register suggests, by Mr. Byron.

In the interim, however, there was much trouble. The lines quoted elsewhere tell us how

> " The Protestant and Schismatick
> Fell out about a candlestick,
> The Father, Sister, Son and Brother
> Fought till they'd ruined one another."

This is supposed to have had reference to the Chandelier dated 1731, of which we can glean little beyond the fact of its purchase.

In July, 1731, Messrs. Shirt and Wainwright go to Ashton-under-Lyne when they "spent on ye road to Ashton and our dinners and spent on Mr. John Barber (one of ye Protestes) and on John Taylor when we made an agreement with him to exchange our candlestick—our horses and ye ostler 12/-."

The story is that this Mr. John Barber, Mr. Thornhill, of the Warmbrook family, and a Mr. Lingard with others interested in the parish, opposed the hanging of the chandelier in the Church on the ground that it was "Popish," and considerable litigation ensued in which the three gentlemen named lost large sums of money.

There is no doubt that at this period there were a number of lawsuits in which one Joseph Trickett was a leading protagonist. He was nephew of Adam Young of Malcalf, and is said to have been engaged in business and to have been connected with a mill, some slight remains of which are still to be seen at the brookside below Malcoff, as we now call the place. He made and spent a good deal of money—not a little it is feared in futile litigation. Amongst other transactions he acquired the Warmbrook estate on the downfall of the Thornhills, but himself eventually became bankrupt, his only record now being "Trickett Lane," above Blackbrook.

He first appears as entering a caveat in the Capitular Court against the election of Jasper Frith and John Wainwright in 1732, when a fee of two guineas was paid by the Wardens "to Mr. Hand for attending ye Court to justifie ye election of ye present Churchwardens, not withstanding Joseph Trickett's caveat."

Although they successfully upheld their election they were again attacked the next year on their accounts, and in spite of their plea that these accounts had been duly presented and approved by the Vestry the Dean ordered them to account again. Messrs. Frith and Wainwright, however, refused to obey, and in Michaelmas Term, 1734, obtained a Writ of Prohibition in the High Court setting

aside the Judgment in the Court at Lichfield. In the
quaint legal language of the day this document states :

"William Bagshaw, Edmund Waterhouse, Joseph
Trickett, John Barber and Thomas Slack well knowing
the premises aforesaid but intending unduly to vex
oppress and weary the said Jasper Frith and John
Wainwright contrary to law and also to disinherit Us
and our Royal Crown and the conusance of a plea
(which specially belongeth and appertaineth to Us and
our Royal Crown)"

had taken proceedings and proceeds to prohibit that
Court from making any order, and if any sentence of
Excommunication against Frith and Wainwright had
been pronounced it was to be immediately revoked.
These gentlemen, who no doubt considered the Church
to be the Servant of the State, would hardly be able to
appreciate the humour of themselves being thus over-
ruled by what some modern Churchmen would call an
Erastian Justiciary, but the fact remains that the case of
Wainwright v. *Bagshaw* is still quoted by ecclesiastical
lawyers as deciding that Churchwardens cannot be called
on to furnish accounts if they have already laid them
before the Vestry.[1] An old paper gives the names of
those who agreed in writing to contribute towards the
costs. In addition to those named in the Prohibition
are Arnold Kirk, Thomas Kirk, Dr. Clegg and William
Barber. Others who "promised only" are Thomas
Mellor, Mr. Mills (agent for Mr. Degge, the owner of
the Bowden Hall estate), John Bagshaw, Josiah Bradbury and Thomas Waterhouse. The Bill of costs of
Mr. Fletcher, paid in 1737, came to over £200, and Mr.
Trickett's account for horse hire and expenses of journeys, etc., came to £143 19s. 11d. more. These heavy

---

1. Phillimore's *Ecclesiastical Law*, 2nd ed., 1487. The case is reported in 2 Stra. 974.

EIGHTEENTH CENTURY LITIGATION

expenses must have covered other litigation to which we shall presently refer, for the Wardens only paid out of Church expenses £19 14s. 6d. to Mr. Mundy, "a Solicitor or Agent for the late officers of ye Parishioners." Mr. Mundy's name appears on the Writ of Prohibition. The good Doctor, like many others who rush heedlessly into law, often in spite of the protests of their advisers, lost his temper when the bill came in. He says "Went up to Chapple to settle matters with him (Mr. Fletcher) about ye Lawsuits, had some hott words with him about his bill, which cost me much concern after. I have not that rule over my own spirit that I recommend to others. May God teach me more meekness and humility and watchfulness." Clegg speaks of further trouble in 1735, but we have no reference to it beyond the entry in his Diary on 17th July, which was the usual time for the Annual Visitation, "Set out with Mr. Kelsal for the Visitation (at Tideswell). Got our business dispatched forthwith. Went up to ye Church. Mr. Green preached a good sermon. Our parish had a long trial about Churchwardens and our friends lost it. The ancient custom was broke through by ye Dean against all right and law."

Mr. Trickett next turned his attention to the Minister, Mr. Bardsley, whom he prosecuted "for immoralities," a proceeding evidently unpopular, for when Trickett was defeated, on account, as he alleged, of the perjury of one of his witnesses, there was "wild and wicked rioting and revelry at Chapel."

Still unsatisfied, Trickett took further action at the Summer Assizes in 1738, and was again unsuccessful, for Dr. Clegg records on July 25th "this night we hear we have lost ye cause at Derby," and the next evening "all the town of Chapel full of rioting and drunkenness on account of their victory at Derby." We do not learn what the trouble was about, and it is best perhaps not to seek to draw the veil, but it is only fair to say that

Trickett's actions seem to have been as unpopular with his friends as with the Minister's supporters. Dr. Clegg says that the suit commenced contrary to the advice of all Trickett's friends: "This I fear may be of bad consequence to ye dissenting interest in these parts," and again, "I could have wished he had not began it: it creates much ill will tho' no dissenter besides has any concern in it." Finally: "I paid to the full this night all my share of the costs and charges of the parish suits, being in all above £27 and am fully determined never more to engage in any suits"; a very wise resolve.

Although Dr. Clegg assisted the parochial litigation by his subscriptions, he was evidently on quite good terms with the clergy, for he attended both the elder Mr. Byron (at whose funeral in 1727 he was a bearer) and Mr. Bardsley in his medical capacity, and assisted the latter's son to obtain a scholarship at Christ Church, Oxford, and, as we have seen, Mr. Byron, Junior, entered into a bond to ensure his receiving part of the Barber money. The Diary also shows that he did his best by discussion with the Minister and others to "accommodate the controversies in the parish," but apparently at the moment without success. But he perhaps paved the way for Mr. Byron, by whose intercession the Parish Register tells us, were terminated the litigious disputes in which the parishioners were engaged at the time of his appointment.

BRIEFS.

Briefs were Letters Patent issued by the Crown authorising the collection of alms in churches for the special objects named therein, chiefly for the repair of churches or the losses sustained by the inhabitants of some parish caused by some calamity, but occasionally for very curious purposes. As a rule very small sums were collected, and during the eighteenth century they were so numerous as to become a nuisance.

The Churchwardens of Chapel obtained a Brief for

the repair of the Church in 1731 ; there is, however, no account of the amount obtained. The Parish Church of Chatham records a collection on this Brief on Sept. 12th, 1731, of 3s. 9¾d.

In the contract with George Platt of Thriber, Yorkshire, Mason, dated 25th July, 1731, the Rev. Benjamin Bardsley, Minister of Chapel, German Buxton of Eccles, John Carrington of Bugsworth, John Frith of Bagshaw, John Barber of Malcalf, Samuel Kirk of Whitehough, and Henry Lomas of Ryeflatt, all described as " gentlemen," are stated to be the Acting Trustees appointed by His Majesty's most gracious Letters Patent to see that the moneys to be collected on Briefs for that purpose then issued were effectually applied in rebuilding the Parish Church and Steeple of Chapel-en-le-Frith.

On this day the Churchwardens " spent at Sealing ye Articles for ye Steeple with Trustees and several freeholders 12/-."

Platt was to be paid £8 per superficial foot measured on the outside of the steeple by two instalments of £50 each and the balance (if any) within a month after completion £10 10s. 0d. for the pinnacles, and £5 5s. 0d. further if the stairs and all other work were done to the " satisfaction of the said trustees or honestly and workmanlike, to be referr'd to men of Judgment."

Our first register contains an account of moneys collected on Briefs from 1660 onwards. The amounts vary from 10d. on August 27th, 1691, for loss by fire at Morpeth in Northumberland to £2 13s. 0d. collected in April, 1688, for French Protestants, two collections for Irish Protestanst £2 7s. 4d. in Oct., 1689, and £1 0s. 3¾d. in the March following, being the next largest amounts. A curious item is 3s. 8d. collected in the Parish on 18th May, 1693, " for the Royal Theatre near Russell St. in the Parish of St. Martins in the Fields London." Drury Lane Theatre and sixty houses had been destroyed by fire in 1672.

The Wardens' Accounts show that the accounts of moneys received on Briefs were balanced up twice a year and the amounts accounted for at the Visitation, the Wardens making the usual charges for expenses. Briefs were finally abolished in 1828.

Rushbearing.

We have noticed in the Churchwardens' Accounts payments made in connection with the annual ceremony of Rushbearing, and also that in the early part of the last century the Church was strewn with rushes. An old parishioner has described to us how in his youth the custom was still kept up. Rushes were then fetched from Rushop and the Poors Piece by the school children and others and carried in procession through the streets with a band and Morris dancers to the Church and there spread in "the middle Aisle," where they remained for a week.

INDEX.

Names given in lists in the body of the work and some others are omitted from this Index for lack of space.

Advowson, claims to, 37, 46 *et seq.*, 64, generally, 39, 46.
Altar rails, Brass, 34, Jacobean, 12, 21.
Apprentices, parish, 100.
Architecture, fourteenth century, 14, Georgian, 17.
Armitage, T. (1434), 78, 79, (1534) 59, 72, 80.
Ashbourne, derivation of, 40, Lane, 40.
Ashton, fam., 50, deed of, 20.
Badgers heads, 98, 99.
Bagsha, Stephen, 20, 78, 80.
Bagshawe, Sir Ed., 72, Geoffrey, 79, (of Ford Hall) Mr. Ernest, 22, 25, 125, Samuel, 27, Rev. Wm., 56, Rev. Wm., M.A., 25, 83, Rev. Wm. (Apostle of the Peak) 82, 113, 117, 152, W. H. G., 26, W. M. C. G., 25.
„ (of Hollin Knowle) Grace 115, Robt. 149.
„ (of Marsh Green) George 149, Robt. 149.
„ (of Ridge Hall) Thomas 16, 70.
Baptism, rights of, conferred on Chapel, 39, 44.
Baptisms in P. R., 112 *et seq.*
Baptistery, 21.
Barber, Hy., 143, John (1731) 153, John (Organist) 11, 143, William, 33, 152.
Bardsley, Rev. B. 24, 73, 74, 128.
Barney, Fras. 62, 67, 81, Thos. 62, 67, 81.
Bassano, notes on Bowden Tomb, 16.
Bassoon, 137.
Bass Viol, 138.
Bayley, Mrs., 35.
Beard, Wm., Quaker, 150.
Bell, Curfew, 136; Great 132, Passing, 136, Sanctus 19, 133. Shrove Tuesday 136, Sunday 136.
Bells, Chapter X., Inscriptions, weights, etc., 133, when formerly rung, 135.
Bellott (Bealot) fam. 28, 50, Abraham 114, Anthony 28, 114.
Benefice, style of, 45, now a Vicarage, 46, 50.
Bennet, John, will of, 20, 33.
Bennett, Ellin, 31, (of Stodhart) 22, John, 35, (of Wellclose) 22, 24, Norman, 22, 24, Robt., 22.
Black Monday, 114.
" Borough," Chapel-en-le-Frith a, 41.
Boundaries of Parish, 42.
Bowden Chapel, 2, 38, 40, 43.
„ the men of, 36, 48, (of Bowden Hall) Nich., 16, 124, George, 124, Jonathan, 150, Thos., 110.
„ Quire, 16, Tomb 16, 22—128.
Bowles MSS., 79, 80.
Bramwell (Bramal) fam., 50, 109, George 100, James 109, Joseph 109, Peter (Parish Clerk) 108, Peter (Sexton) 109, Tom 26, 109.
Bray, Rev. Wm., 81, 110.
Bredbury, Sir Jno., 20.
Brecks, price of, 106.
Brief for rebuilding Church, 19, 157.
Briefs, collections on, 156.
Brockylhurst, Jone, (will of) 57, 122, Oliver (will of) 122.
Browne, fam. 70, Ric. 39, Nich. (1491) 58, Nich. (1523) 80, Nich. (1618) 70.
Bull Ring, 1.

INDEX

Bull's Head Inn, 7, 77.
Burgage tenure, 41.
Burial, rights of, confered on Chapel, 39, 44, places, plan of 125, 127.
Burials, P.R., 115 *et seq.* in Church 115, 122, in woollen 117, at Slack Hall, 117, of non-parishioners 115, 122.
Burrfields, Boroughfields, 41.
Burying cakes, 34.
Butler, Mrs., 11.
Buxton, German, 132.
Byron, Rev. Jno. (1717-27) 60, 73, 82, (1748-90) 34, 74, 83, 114, 152, 156.
"Camera Regia in Foresta Pecci," 39.
"Candlestick," 97, 152, 153, verses on 152.
Carriers to London, 119.
Carrington, James, 139.
Cattle plague, 102.
Causeway, the, 116.
Cavendish, fam. 56.
Chancel, antiquity of, 9, 12, liability to repair, 46, meetings, etc., in, 146, old seats faced west, 130, rebuilding of, 13.
Chandelier, 21, 24, opposition to, 152.
Chapel-en-le-Frith, first mention of, 43, etymology of, 43.
Chaplain, *capellanus* defined, 44.
Charities, 33.
Charles II., appreciation of in P.R., 116.
Child apprentices, 100.
Chimes, the, 35.
Chinley, burial of inhabitants at Chapel, 123.
„ small tithes and Easter offerings, 54.
Church, the, Chap. II., Architecture, 9, Gifts to, 33, memorial windows and monuments, 22, oak altar rails, 12, 21, old painting of, 11, Plate, 35, Reports on condition of (1889), 9, South side rebuilt, 17, stone coffin in, 28, use for secular purposes, 146.
Church officials, Chap. VII.
Churchwardens, list of, 85, accounts, 93, action against, 153, Expenses on Sacramental Days, 95.
Churchyard, 29, gravestones in, 30, old fair-ground adjoining, 7, 32, old houses adjoining, 32.
Clegg, Dr. Jas., 151, 152, Diary of, 7, 113, 118, 151, 155, Friend of incumbents, 156, views on litigation, 156.
Clerks, parish, 107.
Coffin, stone, 28.
Committee of Twenty-seven, 73, their authority doubted, 75, co-opt new members, 75, still appointed on vacancy in benefice, 77.
Cook, Rev. Caleb, 15, 60, 73, 82.
Cooper, Wm., burned to death, 118.
Counsel's opinion on mode of Election of Incumbent, 75.
Coup(er), Hochor, Rich., Thos., 58.
Cox, Rev. J. Charles, 5, 17, 18, 24, 36, 42, 57, 129.
Cresswell, Rev. Edw., 45, 49, 62, 81, John, 58, Nich. (1491) 58, Nich. (will of) 34.
Crist Quarry, 13.
Crossby, Brass, 119.
Darbyshire, Alfred, F.I.B.A., 12.
Dean's or Dane's Yard, 6.
Dedication of Church, 5, date of, 5, 42.
De la Ford, Margery, 57, Nich., 39.
Devonshire, Earl of, 93, Duke of, 54.
Dickie, Professor A. C., opinion of, 13.
Dicson (Dixon), Nich., 79.
Dockyard or Woolcroft, 7.
Domesday Survey, 2.
"Dominus," use of term, 69.

INDEX

Donative, benefice said to be, 45.
Drink, for Ringers, 101, for Singers, 137, for Workmen, 101, 103, 105.
Earthquake recorded in P.R., 120.
Easter offerings, 51.
"Ellin's Grave," 31.
Epidemic disease, evidence of, 113.
Eston, Adam de, 37.
Fairs on Holy Days, 7.
Fernilee, 42, 45, 55.
Ferrars. Robert de, 37, Wm. de, 36, 37.
Font, the, 21, adventures of, 131, basin used as, 21.
Ford, fam. 135.
Forest, meaning of, 43, of High Peak, 1, 43. wastes, 43.
Fox (of Martinside), Adam, 7, 31.
Foxes' heads, payments for, 98, 99, 107.
Frith, Jasper, 20, 74, 152, 153. John, 35. 104, John (Bagshaw) 57, Saml., 139.
Gale, a great, 118.
Gallery, East, 143, west, 137, 138.
Garland in Church, 101.
Gaskell, Fras., charity of, 33. 61.
Gasquet, Cardinal, 44, 121.
Gee, Rev. John, 139, Ralph, 124, Rev. Robt., 81.
Georgian Architecture, 17.
Gibb (Gybbe) fam. 64, Hugh (1423) 64, (1491) 58, Robt. 64.
Gisborne, Thos., M.P.. 54, Walter J., 130.
Given, Rev. Jas., 25, 27, 84.
Glossop parish, 2.
Glover, Stephen, Historian of Derbyshire, 11, 17.
Good Friday, Holy Communion on, 95.
Goodman, fam., 27, Geo., 75, 138, Col. G. D., 85, 92, 125, Thos., 77. 130, Davenport, 92, Thos. D., 26, 143.
Graves, in Church, 115, 122, Plan of, 125, 127, inscriptions on, 30.
Great tithes, 53, 54.
„ War, Roll of the Fallen, 23.
Greaves, Mr. and Mrs. H. M., 25.
Grey. Rev. the Hon. Fras., 130.
Grundy, Rev. Saml., 25, 75, 76, 83.
Hall, Rev. Geo., 25, 76, 84, 143.
Hall, the (Roebuck Inn) 63, 115, 151.
Hallam, Thos., 31.
Hamlets in parish, 1251, 53.
Handel, performance of works of, 140, 144.
Hautboy, 138.
Hearse, parish, 105, house, 105.
Hedgehogs, payments for, 96, 98, 99, 107.
Henry, King, II., 5, III., 37, 38.
Heriots, 57.
Hibbert fam., 135.
Hill. Alf., Builder, 9, 12.
Hiring servants in Churchyard, 7.
Holy Communion, celebration of, 95. on Good Friday. 95, allowance to wardens, 95.
Hope, Church and parish, 2, 4, 42, 44, 47, 51.
Hordern, Horderon, 50.
Horsendon, Wm. de, Bailiff of High Peak, 41.
Inns, Bull's Head, 7. 77, Roebuck, 7. 63, 151, Royal Oak. 63, 73. 95, Thorn Tree, 29, Townhead (King's Arms) 94, 98, Swan, 7.
Inquest *ad quod damnum*, 38, 44, 47, 49.
Instrumental music in choir, 137, 143.
Inscriptions on graves, 30, rafters, 15, roof, 20.
Jagger, John, 24

INDEX

John, King, 3, 37, 40, 46.
Judas Maccabeus performance of, 140.
Kerkyard, Wm. on le, 39, 50.
Kimberley, Dean, 73.
Kirke, Agnes, 147, Arnold (1634) 150, (1732) 154, Helena, 80, Hy. (1841) 25, Hy. (1660) 124, Hy., M.A., 7, Nich., 10, Rich., 80, Saml., 74, Thos., 81.
Kyrke, Thos., will of, 122.
Lancaster, Duchy of, 19, 50.
Land lays, 93.
Langdendale, 2, 36.
"Last Supper," picture of, 24.
Law-suit, witnesses examined in Church, 146.
Lead, price of, 103.
Lenton, Priory of, 3, 36, 37, 39, 46, 51, 53, 64.
Leystalls, 123.
Lichfield, Dean and Chapter of, 3, 37, 39, 46, 52, 57, 62, 64, 70, 71, 72, 74.
„ Dean attends election of minister, 73.
Lime-trees planted, 104.
Linen, burying in, 104.
Lingard fam., 30, Mr. (1731) 153, Quakers, 150.
Litigation in Eighteenth Century, 150.
Lomas, Abraham, 143.
Lowe, fam., 22, John, 7.
"Major and senior part of parishioners," 72.
Marchenton, Elias de, 41, Robt. de, 41.
Marchington, John, 76, Philip, 76.
Marriage, Registers, 114, by J.P., 115, ceremony repeated, 115.
Marshall, Thos., charity of, 33.
Mellor, fam., 148-9, Geo., 72, 81, Hy., 149, Robt., 58., Thos. (1616) 149, Thos. (1734) 154, Widow, 150.
Middleton, John, 60, Robt., 60, Robt. (1778) 141.
Messiah performance in Church, 140.
Ministers, Chap. VI., List of, 79, Election of (1717) 73, (1727) 73, (1747) 74, (1836) 76, (1901) 77, Income, 51, 58, 61, residences, 60.
Morris Dancers, 104, 158.
Mortaigne, John, Earl of, 3, 46, 51.
Mortuaries, 57.
Moult (Mould) fam., 70, Robt. (1345) 50, Robt. "married his wife," 114, Thos. (1618) 70, 85, Thos (tombs of) 31, 128.
Music and singing, Chap. XI.
Nabbs, Rev. Fras., 82.
Names, of Early inhabitants, 41, 50, in First Register, 111.
Nave, 12, 13, arcades, 13, 14, floor raised, 12, roof, 14.
Needham, Saml. (of Lower Eaves), 26, 27, 35, 145, Saml. (of Rushop), 26, 131, (of Perry), 128.
New Chapel of Shallcross, 113.
Nicholas, Quire of St., 16, 127.
Nickson, Rev. Edmund, 75, 81, 123.
Non-parishioners, burial in Church, 115, 122.
Nutting on Sunday, 102.
Oliver, Rev. W., 81.
Oratorios in Church, 140, verses on, 141.
Organ, appeal for funds, 138, specification of first, 139, new chamber, 145.
Organists, 135, 143, 145, salary, 135, 142, 145.
Painting, Mediæval, 10, by John Taylor, 11.
Parish, apprentices, 100, boundaries of, 42, Clerks, 107.
„ Registers, Chap. VIII.
„ Rents paid on morrow of Holy Thursday, 41.
Parliamentary Commission, 1650, 45.

Parsonage, old, 60.
Patronal Festival, 5.
Peak Forest, the, 1, 36, Parish of, 39.
" Peculiar Jurisdiction " of Dean and Chapter, 48, 49.
Pegge, Rev. S., visit to Church, 129.
Penance letter, 98.
Penny Hill, 7.
Petition, Rev. E. Cresswell's, 62. Parishioners', 65.
Peverel, Wm., 3, the younger, 36, 37, 51, 53.
Pews and seats, Chap. IX., Agreements as to, 123, allotment of, 128, 130, old, gorgeous, 129, old oak sent to Buxton, 130, Rents, 125, 139, right to particular, 121, 124, 130. (And see *Seatlays*.)
Phillipa, Queen, nominates a Chaplain, 47.
Phœnix, girl lost in snow, 118.
Pickford, Cornelius (1750) 10, (1790) 108, Jas. (1701) 16, 108. 132, Jas. (1735) 108.
Pictures formerly in Church, Last Supper, 24. Moses and Aaron, 102, Mediæval frescoes, 10.
Pink, Rev. S. H., 22, 84.
Piscena, ancient, 10, 12.
Plan, of graves, 19, 21, 30, 31, 125, 127, Elizabethan, 2, 18.
Plate, Church, 35.
Platt, George, Contractor, 19, 157.
Pleas, at Derby, 37, 47, Forest, 41.
Poors Piece, 56.
Presentation, Evidence of method of, 63, 65, 71, Parishioners' right of, 46, Admitted by Dean and Chapter, 72, Effect of P.C.C. Measure, 1921, on, 76, Counsel's opinion, 75.
Priaccor water, 116.
Priest's door, 10, 11.
Pulpit, 21, 128.
Quaker, burial-place, 117, recusants, 148.
Quire, Bowden or St. Nicholas, 16, 127, Our Lady's, 17, 20, 128.
Rates collected in Churchyard, 7.
Ravens, payments for, 98, 99.
Rawlins, Rev. R. R., remarks on pews, 129.
Receipt Roll, Chapter, 57.
Recusants, 148.
Registers, Parish, Chap. VIII.
Religious census, 1677, 150.
Repewing, 1827, names of Committee for, 130.
Reynolds' notes, 16, 27.
Reckman on 14th Century Architecture, 14.
Ringers, the, Chap. X., wages, 134.
Roads, ancient, 1, 40.
Roebuck Inn, 7, 63, 151.
Royal Oak Inn, 63, 73, 95.
Rudhall, Abm., 133, 134.
Rushbearing, 94, 104, 107, 158.
Rushes in Church, 106, 129, 158.
Sanctus Bell, 19, 133.
Scholes, Elizabeth, charity of, 33.
School sermons, 144.
Scottish prisoners in Church, 18, 147.
Seat lays, 93, 128, assessment list, 17, 20, 125
Seats, allotment of (1834), 129.
Secular purposes, use of Church for, 146.
Sermons, School, 144, " trial," 77.
Sextons, list of, 109.
Shallcross, John (1624) 113, John (1712) 8, 16.
,, Chapel at, 113, tithes, 43.
Shirt, Dorothy, charity of, 34, John, 24, 153.

INDEX

Shrewsbury, Eliz. Countess of, 47, 56, 64, Earl of, 148.
Singers, loft, 137, payments to, 137, visits of neighbouring, 138
Slack, Mrs., 26, of Tideswell, 143, Thos., 154.
Small tithes, 54.
S.P.A.B., 12.
Stained glass, modern, 22.
Stavenby, Alex., Bishop of Lichfield, 3, 42, 44, 45, 48.
Steeple, the, 18, 19, 128.
Stipend, minister's, 58.
Stredder, Rev. J. C., 12, 35, 84.
Sun-dial (1733), 17, in Churchyard, 32.
Survey of Chapter Estates, 1650, 59.
Sydebotham, Robt. de, 49, 57.
Taylor, fam., 21, 50, Fras., 149, John, 11.
Thomas of Canterbury, St., 4.
Thorn Tree Inn, stone coffin at, 29.
Thorneley, Matilde de, 41.
Thornhill v. Tooker, 4, 49, 62 *et seq.*, 146.
Thornhill, fam., 50, Geo., 64, Geo. (1634) 149, Mr., 153.
Tideswell, 3, 52, 143.
Tithe Barn, the, 6.
Tithes in Chapel, 4, 45, 51, 93, in Fernilee, 43, 45.
,, Peverel's grant of, 3, 51.
Tooker, Dean, 62, 66, 67.
Townhead (King's Arms Inn), 94, 98.
Tower built, 157.
Town-planning, Mediæval, 40.
Townstall, case of, 44, 48.
Tragedies recorded in P.R., 115.
Trees planted in Churchyard, 104.
Trickett, Jos., 153 *et seq.*
Tuesday, association of, with St. Thomas of Canterbury, 5.
Twenty-seven, the Committee of, 73, 75, 77.
Vermin, payments for destruction of, 96, 98, 99, 107.
Verses, anonymous, 141.
Vestry meetings in Church, 146.
Wages of Workmen, 99, 102. (And see Churchwarden's accounts, *passim*.)
Wainwright, John, 20, 151, 153.
Wainwright v. Bagshaw, 154.
Wakes, the, 5, origin of, 6.
"Walking in Church," 100.
Walker, Harold H., 26.
Ward, Gaul H., 20, Geo., 127.
Wastes, Forest, 43.
White, Rev. Wm., 21, 60, 73, 82, Edw., 24.
,, bread, 34, Sunday, 114.
Wittenbury, C., report by, 12.
"Widow and Spinster," 115.
Wigan, great bell re-cast at, 132.
Wills—Barber, Wm., 33, 152; Bennet, John, 20, 33; Brockylhurst, Jone, 122, Oliver, 122; Cresswell, Nichs., 34; Gaskell, Fras., 33; Kyrke, Thos., 122; Marshall, Thos., 33; Scholes, Eliz., 33.
Windows, ancient, 11, clerestory, 14, memorial, 22.
Wine, price of, 94.
Wool Fair, the, 5.
Wormhill, 2, 24.
Yeaveley, fam., 63, Rev. Geo., 63, 69, 72.
Young, Adam, 153.

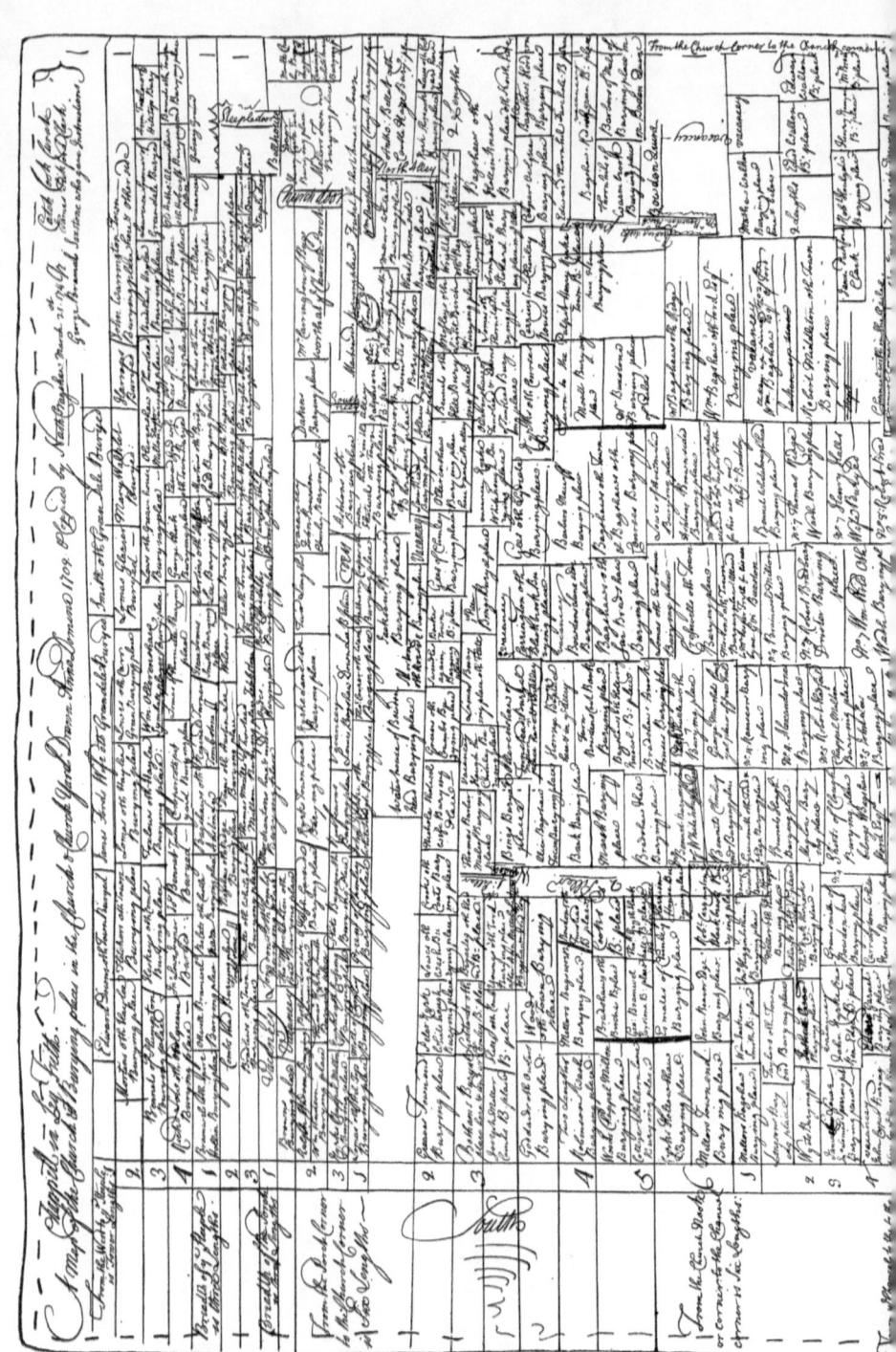

www.ingramcontent.com/pod-product-compliance
Lightning Source LLC
Chambersburg PA
CBHW030323080526
44584CB00012B/680